M000031867

Filling the God–Shaped Void

A Book of
DAILY MEDITATIONS

PENNY MARY HAUSER, MSN

Liguori
LIGUORI, MISSOURI

Imprimi Potest:
Harry Grile, CSsR, Provincial
Denver Province, The Redemptorists

Published by Liguori Publications
Liguori, Missouri 63057

To order, call 800-325-9521
www.liguori.org

Copyright © 2012 Penny Mary Hauser

All rights reserved. No part of this publication may be reproduced, stored in a retrieval system, or transmitted in any form or by any means—electronic, mechanical, photocopy, recording, or any other—except for brief quotations in printed reviews, without the prior written permission of Liguori Publications.

Library of Congress Cataloging-in-Publication Data
Hauser, Penny Mary.
    Filling the God-shaped void : a book of daily meditations / Penny Mary Hauser. — 1st ed.
        p. cm.
    1. Church year meditations. 2. Spiritual life—Meditations. 3. Lord's prayer—Meditations. 4. Christian life—Catholic authors—Meditations. I. Title.
    BX2170.C55H38 2012
    242'.3—dc23

                                                                        2012018232
pISBN: 978-0-7648-2162-2
eISBN: 978-0-7648-6727-9

Scripture quotations are from *New Revised Standard Version Bible,* copyright © 1989 National Council of the Churches of Christ in the United States of America. Used by permission. All rights reserved.

Excerpts from the English translation of *The General Instruction of the Roman Missal* from *The Roman Missal* © 2010, International Commission on English in the Liturgy Corporation. All rights reserved.

Compliant with *The Roman Missal,* third edition.

Liguori Publications, a nonprofit corporation, is an apostolate of The Redemptorists. To learn more about The Redemptorists, visit Redemptorists.com.

Printed in the United States of America
16 15 14 13 12 / 5 4 3 2 1
First Edition

Dedication

To Linda, a spiritual hero,
who lives in the promises of Christ

Acknowledgments

As is often said in these meditations, the Holy Spirit nudges, teaches, inspires, grounds us, and provides all good things in our lives. The Spirit comes into our lives through amazing circumstances and amazing people. My deepest thanks go to Ivy for the gentle nudges; to Joe for the teaching and grounding in my daily journey of faith; to Karen for the edits and "messing around" with the words. This book never would have happened without each of you. Blessings.

Contents

Easter: Jesus' Resurrection in Our Lives

Post-Pentecost: The Holy Spirit Within Us

Understanding Jesus: How Can We Be Apostles?

The Power of Prayer

Advent/Christmas: Season of Hope

Introduction

"There is a God-shaped void in the heart of every man which cannot be filled by any created thing but only by God, the Creator, made known through Jesus Christ."

—BLAISE PASCAL 1623–1662

Thanks for picking up this book. What you'll soon realize is that this is not a book filled with answers. This is a book that considers ideas, conversations, and questions that strive to reassure and challenge us about the everyday anxieties of our lives. The readings attempt to share thoughtful perspectives on our day-to-day challenges as spouses, parents, employees—ordinary people searching for a closer relationship with Christ.

The readings are structured in fifty-two weeks. These weeks loosely follow the various parts of the Church year. But because Easter, for example, is a movable feast and Christmas falls on different days of the week, there is no absolute calendar to follow here. Rather, you'll find certain themes and challenges central to strengthening our relationship with God throughout the entire year. The themes touch on such topics as transforming our lives, empowerment through the Holy Spirit, and God's promises. Because of my personal journey and my work in the field of addiction, I also emphasize the challenges of recovery. Since we all have addictions, attachments, and priorities that interfere with our journey toward Christ, please translate *addiction* to any of your own challenges.

You can pick any week to begin your reading. Each week starts with a brief Scripture quote that focuses the week. The Scripture quote is followed by a Sunday devotion. These Sunday devotions come from the many discussions I've had over the years at church, in Bible studies, from my readings and personal reflections. The Monday-through-Saturday meditations consider how the Scripture readings and Sunday devotions pertain to and intersect with our lives. How do we move into a meaningful life centered through Jesus Christ in a relationship with God—a relationship in which we trust his promise to always be with us; and how do we respond to his promise of forgiveness and peace?

My prayer for you as you consider these readings is that the Spirit of God will enliven your faith, strengthen your trust, and increase your love for God. May the empowerment of the Holy Spirit also increase your love for all the people who intersect with your life as you journey toward filling the God-shaped void and experiencing the abundant life God promises.

Week 1:
Epiphany: A Different Way Home

In the time of King Herod, after Jesus was born in Bethlehem of Judea, wise men from the East came to Jerusalem, asking, "Where is the child who has been born king of the Jews? For we observed his star at its rising, and have come to pay him homage."–MATTHEW 2:1–2

Sunday • Shortly after the beginning of the New Year comes Epiphany, which has to do with revelation, with manifestation. But manifestation of what? As one of the hymns points out, "God in man made manifest." God comes in human form.

The Wise Men followed the star and visited the Christ Child. In doing this, they encountered God in this infant named Jesus. They knelt and were face-to-face with God.

One of the things I find really interesting about this incident is how the Wise Men returned by a different way, by another route. The point of application to our lives is obvious. We have just celebrated Christmas—the remarkable story of God in a manger; but if we go back the same way, if it left us unchanged in direction and goals and behavior and speech, then why did we bother coming in the first place? Why did we celebrate Christmas? Was it to find a different way home to God?

If we wise men and wise women come to Jesus' manger with open hearts and willingness to give ourselves to Christ, we will find peace. No matter what we bring with us—sin and guilt, worries and anxieties, all our weaknesses and defeats—we will receive an epiphany, a revelation. We will know we are forgiven. We will not go away empty-handed!

Monday • The feast of Epiphany falls on the first Sunday after January 1. I celebrated Epiphany one year with a friend who had recently dealt with the illness and death of her husband. The Christmas tree and the manger were still up in the church, and the figures of the Wise Men were placed close to the manger but not quite there yet. For this friend, the whole season of Christmas felt like it had not occurred, and she was confused as to why the celebration was still going on.

That happens for a lot of us. Once Christmas day is over, the tree comes down and we begin preparing for New Year's parties, football, skiing, and fun. We forget the Greatest Birthday Party ever celebrated and what it might mean in our lives.

On this first week of the New Year, let's spend some time looking at what Christ's birth might mean in our lives. Does it make any difference?

Tuesday • At this Epiphany service with my friend, the priest invited the children to the altar to move the Wise Men up to the manger. Before allowing them to move the figures, he asked the children, "Who is in the stable?" The usual answers of "Mary and Joseph and the angels and the shepherds" were given. And then one little girl said, "I was there." Isn't that one of the most remarkable responses you've ever heard? A parent or grandparent or teacher had presented such a clear picture of the miracle of Christ's birth that this little girl actually saw herself in that scene. She, like all young children, knew the importance of her own birthday, so naturally Christ's birthday would have been the Greatest Birthday Party ever! And she just knew she had been there.

Were you at the Birthday Party? Was it real for you?

Wednesday • In this first week of the New Year, many of us make a couple of resolutions going forward. Maybe we wrote them down. Maybe we just said them to ourselves in secret. Sharing resolutions is hard because it makes them more real. And if they're real, that means we have to make an effort to keep them. Many of my resolutions are around living more healthfully, losing weight, exercising more, eating better. All of these are reasonable and certainly pertain to using the gifts of our body and health in a way God intends for us to use them.

Some of our resolutions are more spiritually based. At some level we know we want God more present in our lives. We have just witnessed and celebrated Christmas. God became manifest in our lives! A "manifest" for a ship or for an airplane is a document bearing all the names of the passengers who are present on that craft. God being "manifest" in our lives means our names are on Christ's document that says, "I am born into your life, not just at Christmas, but every day of your life."

As you think about resolutions, can you consider ones that would help you know the presence and power of God in your life? Will that knowledge make a difference in your daily decisions?

Thursday • The Wise Men arrived at the stable with gifts of gold, frankincense, and myrrh. Expensive gifts. What do we have that could possibly measure up? As we talked about in the Sunday devotion, what Christ amazingly wants as gifts is our shame, our guilt, our anxieties, our weaknesses, and our defeats. He wants us to turn those burdens over to him. He will change them into forgiveness, peace, and strength. He promises to take the sadness and weariness we are carrying and exchange them for his joy and energy. That is what is celebrated in the birth, life, death, and resurrection of Christ. He forgives us and gives us a life of grace...a life free to know we are beloved. If we are open to the Spirit, if we listen deeply to the whisper of what is being revealed to us daily, then we will know that God is manifest—present—in our lives.

What gift do you have to give to the Christ Child? What sadness, what burden? Is it your anger, your lying, your addictions? Can you pray for openness to God's promise of a new life in this new year?

Friday • The Wise Men had traveled a long way, watching the night skies, until they found their way to the King of the Jews. They were changed by what occurred at the stable as they presented their gifts and worshiped the Christ Child. They were warned in a dream to return to their country by another route, so they changed their direction. Maybe it was for their own safety. Maybe it was to confound the jealous Herod and protect the Child. Their dreams warned them.

Have you ever had a revelation? Mine seem to come very slowly. It seems to take me a long time to recognize a whisper or a warning to change direction. But ultimately when I listen, when my heart is open, when I am more willing to give myself over to Christ, he gives me a new direction; he shows me a different way home to him. But I am the one who has to leave all my unnecessary baggage behind and take that trip.

What differences do you really want in your life? What new routes do you wish to travel? What has to happen for you to set out in the new direction? How will you do that? How will you pray to know God is with you?

Saturday • Taking a different way means we have to get a new map or set our GPS for another destination. And we might think, as Alice did when she searched for Wonderland, "How will I get there if I don't know where I'm going?" It takes creativity and determination.

Taking a different way requires planning. On a new trip, do

we even know where we are going? We have to consider new data and be willing to change our plans. We might have to contact other people along the way, figure out new places to stay, different places to eat, and where to get gas. We think about who to contact for support along the way. On our different way home to God, we will need to be fed and filled spiritually. We might need friendly folks to give us directions. And it's very important to stop along the way to evaluate the progress we are making. We might miss so much if we skip steps or drive too fast.

Our relationship and our connection with God are what make this trip possible. He gives us the strength to continue on this new route. We don't do it ourselves. We don't have to. He promises to be with us...the whole way.

Where are you going? What specific plans do you have to make on your new way home to God? What trusted people can you go to for support? How will your prayer life keep you connected with God?

From Water to Wine: Jesus in Our Lives

The next seven weeks of devotions and meditations discuss Christ's miracle of changing water to wine—a transformational miracle. We discuss the transformational miracle Christ wants to perform in our lives.

Week 2: Signs

On the third day there was a wedding in Cana of Galilee, and the mother of Jesus was there. Jesus and his disciples had also been invited to the wedding. When the wine gave out, the mother of Jesus said to him, "They have no wine." And Jesus said to her, "Woman, what concern is that to you and to me? My hour has not yet come." His mother said to the servants, "Do whatever he tells you."—JOHN 2:1–5

Sunday • Signs point to something. On the highway a sign tells us there is a curve ahead or traffic lights coming up or an intersection at the top of the hill.

John tells us a story about Jesus turning water into wine at a wedding feast. John calls this incident a sign: "Jesus did this, the first of his signs, in Cana of Galilee" (2:11).

That's significant. What is the purpose of a sign? We said it points to something. Jesus turns the water into wine. That's a sign, John says, and it points to something. In this case it points to something extremely important for our lives. It points to Jesus Christ. It says, "Stop...look...listen." It says, "Consider the person who stands before you and knocks on the door of your heart. Consider the person who has come to you clothed in your humanity and wants to be one with you. He is a very special gift from God. He is unique—there is none like him. Stop what you are doing and listen to the word he speaks to you. He can change your life!

Monday • The gospel writer John tells us that this first miracle was a "sign," and Sunday's devotion tells us this sign is significant. A sign says, "Pay attention!" Who, what, when, where, how, and why are the signs in your life. Are they significant? Do they help you to pay attention—to stop...look...listen?

Think about the people who have been "signs" in your own life. Generally our parents are our first giver of "signs." When we become teenagers, we get even more signs from them and our peers. We learn to pay attention to the signs teachers and later bosses and coworkers give us. Even our culture gives us signs. Advertisements give us signs. Churches give us signs—sometimes on billboards outside their front doors.

Symbols are also signs we recognize. Car manufacturers spend millions of dollars so you recognize the symbol of the make of their car—a Mercedes Benz, a BMW, a Chevy, or a Ford. Television stations have signs so you know them automatically by their logos: CBS, NBC, ABC, FOX. You can probably picture their signs just in reading their names.

A cross or crucifix is a powerful sign. What does that sign say?

Who or what gives you the important signs in your life? Is that significant to you? How do you know?

Tuesday • Recently after a major flood, we drove on highways loaded with signs, "Road crews at work." If I didn't pay attention to that message, my car and I would be in big trouble. Stop. Slow. That is the "what" of a road sign.

Significant people in our lives give us messages, often just by the tone of their voice. Do they respect us or dismiss us?

Early signs play a powerful role in who we become, what we believe, and how we behave. In fact, the "what" of messages from parents and teachers and even teenage peers stays with us for the rest of our lives.

It is worthwhile as we mature and gain some perspective on our lives to think through "what" those messages were as we grew up. How did they form us? Did they tell us we were loved and cared for, or did they tell us we were worthless, dumb, or geeks? Once we know the "who" and the "what" of those messages, we can decide to let them have space in our heads or replace them with signs with different messages.

Christ starts his public life with the sign of a transformative miracle: He turns water into wine. The "what" of this sign, the message of this miracle at Cana, is that transformation is ahead—your transformation—stop...look...listen. Pay attention to the guidance he is going to give through his life, death, and resurrection.

What messages from your past guide your life at this point? Do you hear them repeat in your head? Are they messages of affirming love? What message helps you pay attention to the work crew directing you toward a new life in Christ?

Wednesday • In this miracle at Cana, the person, the "who," giving us the sign is Christ. The "what," the message, is pay attention to Christ's life, death, and resurrection. The "when" is now. Pay attention now! It is so easy to be caught up in our own lives. We continue habits and patterns that are destructive or, at the very least, nonproductive. We miss the sign and the message that things can change. God in Christ is with us at each moment of our lives.

When we pay attention to Christ's new message of change, our world can change. Old habits and patterns can be altered. We can begin to respond to people and situations differently.

We can even revise some of the old messages we heard from the past. When we begin to understand that the old destructive messages came from people who were wounded, we begin to replace those messages with Christ's word that he came to give us peace. There is a shift. When we begin to be more mindful of Christ, everything changes. Water becomes wine.

As you move through today, how might you pay more attention to Christ in your life? Can you change your tone of voice when someone irritates you? Can you smile at the cashier in the supermarket? Can you spend an extra minute with your child as you put her to bed?

Thursday • Where? Everywhere! The message is everywhere, in all parts of our lives, if only we will pay attention. Christ is everywhere—are we open to that?

A colleague, who is a counselor in a treatment program for people with addictions, puts it this way. When he goes to the front desk to bring a new client back to his office for an initial interview, he says a prayer that he will be able to see Christ in this client. He says, "I believe Christ is present in each person. Christ comes into this world clothed in our humanity. I just didn't know Christ looks like this sometimes."

When we don't pay attention, we miss Christ in others. Where will Christ be in those you are with today?

Friday • Sometimes Christ gives us his message by knocking directly on our door. He performs a miracle in our lives, and we miss it. It's like we have a peephole in the door, but when we look to see who is there, we see a stranger and refuse to open it.

We miss the everyday miracles of certain people in our lives, the miracle of the change of seasons, the miracle of the birth of a child. A young man recently talked of the birth and growth of his child as the most miraculous thing he's ever seen. His voice was filled with awe and wonder.

In recovery from addictions, people miss the miracle when they don't acknowledge that Christ performed the miracle of recovery in their lives. They think they have done it all themselves. Even if a relapse occurs, it is vital to acknowledge that Christ is with us and will remain with us as we work toward the peaceful life of recovery.

How do you pay attention to the miracles in your daily life? Do you hear the message of those signs—Christ is with you? Do you hear this with awe and wonder?

Saturday • What do think happened when Christ performed this miracle of changing water into wine? I would guess the party took on some new energy. I suspect that guests who were about to leave stayed. Maybe there was more dancing. The party took on new life.

That is what happens when we recognize the miracle of Christ in our lives: we get new energy, there is dancing and new life!

Christ performed the miracle at Cana because he wants to guide us toward a new life. He wants to give us signs and messages that speak to us in loving words and tone. He wants us to know his message will guide us along a sometimes hazardous and dangerous road. And if we pay attention, we will see his message in the daily miracles of our lives. We will hear his knock at the door and he won't be a stranger because we will have paid attention. We will know him and we will let him into our lives.

Why do you pay attention to the signs of Christ's message in your life? What difference does it make when you stop...look... listen to his word of love?

Week 3: Miracles

Jesus said to them, "fill the jars with water." And they filled them up to the brim. He said to them, "Now draw some out, and take it to the chief steward."–JOHN 2:7–8

Sunday • Jesus was at the wedding feast at Cana when the bride and groom ran out of wine to serve the guests. Can you imagine how embarrassed they were? They came up short and felt humiliated.

I know I have behaved in a lot of ways that embarrassed me. But the thing I am most embarrassed by is that I am not the person God intended me to be. I repeatedly come up short. I fail more times than I can count. I am often greedy and selfish and self-serving. I am not what God redeemed me to be.

But look at what happens to the wedding couple. Christ steps in. He changes the water into wine. He covers their embarrassment. And that is exactly what he does for us. He covers our embarrassment with the gracious cover of his love. He doesn't ask us to wallow in shame; he doesn't try to humiliate us by pointing out how we have fallen short of what God wants us to be. Instead he forgives us; he puts his arm around our shoulders and says, "Be of good cheer. I accept you with all your shortcomings."

Monday • There are many reasons for embarrassment. Sometimes it is for something we do unintentionally, like stumbling on a curb or spilling gravy on a white tablecloth. We were probably just not paying close attention to what we were doing. The memory of those times can still make us cringe even years later.

Sometimes the embarrassment is for something more serious. Maybe we have been so absorbed in work that we have forgotten the birthday or anniversary of someone we love. They are hurt, and we are embarrassed. It points out that we have lost focus of what is important.

And sometimes the embarrassment hits us at our core. We are humiliated. Our behavior or our lack of a moral compass or our desire to get ahead has betrayed who we want to be. The humiliation hits us like a blow to the stomach. We almost physically bend over. A tension and anxiety accompany those memories.

The wedding couple was having such a good time, they didn't notice the wine was running low. They were going from table to table, greeting guests and thanking them for their gifts. What would have happened if the wine had run out completely? The party and celebration would have ended, and the guests would have snickered at the poor planning. Fortunately Christ's mother (like all good mothers) was paying attention and knew Christ would help. She knew he would not want the couple to be embarrassed.

So Christ stepped in and turned water into wine, just as he steps into our lives and transforms them with large and small miracles.

When you think of embarrassing moments in your life, what is your gut reaction? Where do you feel the tension and anxiety in your body? Ask Christ to help you release that tension.

Tuesday • The times we are most embarrassed and humiliated are the times we have not lived up to who God intended us to be. That is when the shame is at our core.

When our behavior has shamed us at our core, it is sometimes because of addiction. This can be addiction to anything—work, food, gambling, sex, drugs, alcohol, exercise and weight, shopping. Gerald May, in his book *Addiction and Grace*, says to be human is to be addicted. Others might say addiction is part of the human condition. For me, addiction to alcohol created behaviors that to this day cause me embarrassment, humiliation, and shame. Some of those behaviors were things like laughing too loudly at parties or spilling a drink; but they were also situations of being drunk when the kids came home from school and my precious daughter asking, "What's wrong, Mommy?" And there were times I drove drunk with children in the car. Those are behaviors that continue to haunt me because I know I caused pain and because I know that is not who God redeemed me to be.

When you think of times of embarrassment or humiliation or shame in your life, is it something you can smile about—a minor incident—or is it something that causes you great sadness? Is it a time when you knew you had closed off your relationship with God?

Wednesday • One of the incredible messages we take from this miracle of changing water into wine is that Christ steps into our embarrassment and humiliation and shame. In 1 Peter 4, we read, "Love covers a multitude of sins." A few months after I entered recovery my precious daughter said, "Mommy, you are so nice now that you are not drinking." Her love erased my embarrassment. Love can cover a multitude of sins.

Christ covers our embarrassment and humiliation and shame with his redeeming love. He steps into our lives, and just like a deep, fresh snow, he covers the black and scarlet shame with his gracious love.

When do you feel Christ's gracious love covering your shame?

Thursday • Christ does not want us to remain stuck and wallowing in our humiliation and shame. After all, he gave his life for us to be forgiven and blessed.

When I was drinking, I lived in fear that "someone would know." Someone would figure out I had a problem. Isn't that a hoot? Of course, someone knew. They were just afraid to bring it up. Sadly that reluctance or fear to bring it up just lets the disease progress. Miraculously, truly miraculously, God found a way for me to confront the problem and seek help. He didn't want me to continue to wallow in the guilt, shame, fear, and terror that this disease created. He showed me in his miracles and in his life, death, and resurrection that there was a new way to live. This was "good news"!

Is there an attachment or addiction that keeps you stuck? Is there a new way to think about it, a new way to confront it? Can you pray for God to open you to his message of "good news"?

Friday • When people enter recovery from addictions, we see a physical change in their presence. Of course they look better because the poison has been removed from their bodies. The color in their face returns, they smile, they walk tall. Their whole presence becomes lighter. They begin to talk about hope. That is the miracle of recovery.

An essential part of that miracle also is a sense of forgiveness. Family, friends, and others in recovery give support, and with that support comes new relationships and a sense of forgiveness. That forgiveness may not be spoken in clear sentences, but there is a change in the conversation. It's not about "What's wrong, Mommy?" but "You're so nice."

When the recovering person notices the change and recognizes the change as an openness to God's message of forgiveness, there is a move into longer-term recovery. The relationship with God becomes the sustaining core.

Even if you do not think of yourself as "addicted," is there a part of your life you would like to change or modify? Is there something that causes you anxiety or embarrassment? If you could make some change in that area, would you feel a lightness? Would forgiveness be part of that lighter feeling? Can you be open to your relationship with God as essential to that change?

Saturday • In this miracle of the wedding feast and running out of wine, God shows us he understands that we come up short—many times. We behave and do things that are not what he intends for our lives. But he does not stand there like an angry parent and say, "I told you so." No, he steps in and creates a miracle. He says, "Ok, let's get some fresh water and turn this thing around." It's interesting, too, that he uses water for his first miracle. He also uses water as the first miracle of our lives—baptism. When we are baptized, we are named a blessed child of God.

Loving parents may not like a child's behavior, but they understand that the child is learning. The child may have shortcomings and failures, but loving parents are always there and forgive. Loving parents place their arm around their child's shoulder and say, "I accept you for who you are." When we stumble time after time, that forgiveness is hard to believe. Nevertheless, it's real.

Christ forgives through his life, death, and resurrection. You've already been forgiven! Do you believe it?

Week 4: New Life

When the steward tasted the water that had become wine, and did not know where it came from (though the servants who had drawn the water knew), the steward called the bridegroom and said to him, "Everyone serves the good wine first, and then the inferior wine after the guests have become drunk. But you have kept the good wine until now."–JOHN 2:9–10

Sunday • Jesus' changing the water into wine is a sign that points to a claim he makes about himself. Whenever Jesus comes into a life—any life, even your life—he brings to that life a new quality (like turning water into wine). That's the difference he can make in our lives.

All of us desire a life of highest quality. What we want is not merely to exist or survive; rather, we want a life that is worthwhile—a life that is worth living—a life that is worth getting out of bed in the morning. We want a life that will challenge us and satisfy the deepest regions of our heart.

And Christ gives us that. He does it by transforming our lives, much like the water into wine. The emphasis is on the word *transform*. He is not interested in simply remodeling our lives; he wants to do a major overhaul. He wants to make us a new people with new dreams, new hopes, new values, new behaviors, and new attitudes. He gives us new ways of responding to people. In short, he wants to give us a new way of *living*.

That is why he entered into our human existence and clothed himself in our flesh and blood. That's why he died on the cross feeling forsaken by the Father and reviled by others—and that is why he rose again in triumph. All of this happened so that we could have a life of quality. He did this, and continues to do this, so that we can feel fully alive—new. That is the life he is offering us as a gift. All we need is to open our hearts and our hands.

Monday • Starting in the early 1980s, many organizations initiated a component of responsibility for unit or corporate quality improvement. In the early days of that effort, the term was *quality assurance* and has since morphed to *quality improvement*. Standards and benchmarks were set in organizations as wide-ranging as car manufacturers to health care. As a nurse manager, I was enthusiastic. I viewed quality control as a very good thing since it was clear to me that quality of patient care varied from hospital to hospital and from organization to organization.

However as the years passed, the requirements by licensing and accreditation agencies became onerous. In hospital accreditation and nursing organizations, the time and efforts required by management and staff to meet the paperwork requirements took valuable time away from focusing on patients. Reciting a mission statement rarely transformed the organization.

That is not the way Christ's gracious love is to transform our lives. Transforming our lives is not about crossing the *t*'s or dotting the *i*'s of our religious traditions. It is about accepting the "good news" of Christ's life, death, and resurrection. We are forgiven, loved, and blessed. It is about taking that forgiveness, love, and blessing and living it in our lives with others. That is what improves the quality of our lives. That is what transforms us.

Do you have an area of your life that could use some "quality improvement"? How would that look?

Tuesday • Accreditation agencies set the standards for quality based on a ranking scale. As the efforts changed over the years, the standards moved from "assuring" to "improving." That meant the organization was required to show that it was always improving. For example, simply demonstrating that all charting reflected the patient care plan was not sufficient. We had to prove how physicians, nurses, and techs were improving. That was a good thing. Organizations cannot meet a standard and then rest on their laurels. The quality of the service provided by the organization will slip. There needs to be a constant vigil, and as accrediting agencies evolved, so did their requirements for organizational review and research to demonstrate ongoing improvement efforts.

Our lives also need continued "review" and "research" for ongoing improvement efforts. For our lives to have quality, we have to believe they are worthwhile. If we become complacent, our lives become stagnant. We become restless and bored, even anxious. We can easily move away from the goals we have set as standards. We move away from a life centered in a relationship with Christ.

Do you consider a life based on a relationship with Christ as a life worthwhile? What standards do you name as the criteria for meeting the goal of that worthwhile life?

Wednesday • At the beginning of the "quality assurance" organizational efforts, much of the work was looking at the organization's past performance. Reviewing past incidents was the focus. What had happened? What had gone wrong? In the car industry there was focus on why engines didn't start, why brakes failed, why air bags didn't deploy. In health care we looked at past surgical errors, medication errors, patient falls. But to move organizations into forward-thinking "quality improvement," we had to ask ourselves, "What will improve the quality of patient care?" not just, "What did we do wrong?"

So it is with our lives. Looking at the past and figuring out what is going wrong is a reasonable place to start. But to really move into a life that we know is worthwhile requires moving from the past into new challenges. It means looking at the destructive behaviors and acknowledging those behaviors that keep us stuck. We ask God to be with us; we are able to define new goals, challenges, and standards that we know will transform our lives.

What is one new challenge you can set for yourself today—something that will make you feel your life has meaning? Maybe an extra moment of prayer? Maybe an extra smile and gentle word to a coworker or a person on the bus? Maybe letting someone merge into your lane on the freeway? Something!

Thursday • When I was involved in quality-improvement efforts, I often became frustrated. It seemed no matter how much we refined the paperwork or initiated educational efforts, sometimes the day-to-day patient care didn't improve. Staff could still be rude when answering the phone. They could be short-tempered with patients. They could be chronically late for work. No amount of paperwork or written standards and reports can change organizations; people do—people and their attitudes and their commitment to the organization; people who believe the job they do is worthwhile; people who believe the changes they are asked to make will make a difference.

Often improving the quality of our lives requires not only small changes but major renovations. We have to believe the changes we make will make a difference...to ourselves and to others. Christ is not an accreditation agency, thank God! *Really* thank God! But Christ came so that we can have life and have it abundantly. So we can believe our lives are worthwhile. So we can believe in his gracious love. So we can name the challenges and transform our lives through his grace.

Do you see your life as an accreditation checklist or can you begin to have new dreams of a life of continuing creativity, excitement, and challenge?

Friday • I have a friend who has a lot of change going on in her life. Her youngest son is graduating from high school but hasn't begun to fill out college applications or write the essay. She recently resigned as chair of a committee at work because she believes she cannot ethically be part of the developing politics of the committee. She and her husband are building a new house, but the plans at this point are not what she envisioned. And in all of this she smiles and says, "I'm really curious about how this or that will turn out. I wonder how this will look in a year."

Isn't that a wonderful attitude? She's concerned about all of these issues because they are serious and important. She is not abdicating her role in each situation, but she's not wringing her hands and letting it color every moment of her day. She has this delightful smile and openness and, above all, curiosity.

Wouldn't it be wonderful to bring that attitude into the dreams and challenges of our new lives? Are you curious about what Christ has in store for you?

Saturday • Christ's transformation of the water into wine tells us he is present to transform our lives. After the steward tastes the new wine, he praises the bridegroom for saving the best wine until last. Christ had not just provided more of the same old wine; he'd improved it!

That's what he does in our lives as well. He promises to improve the quality of our lives. He invites us to participate in that improvement by bringing the "water" of our lives to him. He will transform us if we present our lives to him. He works in our lives, and when we "taste" our new lives, we will know he has performed a miracle.

What would it mean to present the water of your life to Christ and ask him to improve it?

Week 5: God's Graciousness

He said to them, "Now draw some out, and take it to the chief steward."–JOHN 2:8

Sunday • When they ran out of wine, we see Jesus covering the wedding couple's embarrassment by changing the water into wine. And we know he covers our embarrassment for consistently falling short of what he wants us to be.

This account shows us another aspect of our Lord's graciousness. He is there to help. He is present when we fail and fall. He knows what we need even before we ask him. The Apostle Paul tells us that God is more ready to give than we are to ask. He is by our side to help us. "The Lord is our refuge...a very present help in trouble" (Psalm 46:1).

Sometimes we think we alone have to make ourselves into the kind of people God wants us to be. If we try hard enough we can measure up to his expectations. A therapist once told me, "Trying is lying." The trouble is, we can't do it ourselves no matter how hard we try—no matter how many resolutions we make.

The good news is we don't have to. Christ is there to help us! He is there to make us new creatures. He is there to mold us into his likeness. All we need to do is let go of what we think we control and allow his powerful and renewing Spirit to fill our hearts and our lives. His name is Emmanuel—God with us.

Monday • What are the characteristics of a person in your life whom you consider "gracious"? It's not necessarily how they behave or what they do. It's more a sense of who they are. Words like gentle, loving, nonjudgmental, and warm come to mind. We think of someone who is gracious as very giving—giving of time and understanding. When we consider the "graciousness" of God, we are saying he is full of grace. He is full of all these things, and he wants to infuse our lives with them.

I have a friend, Rosie, whom I consider to be full of God's grace. She is warm, gentle, loving. Her life is not without strain, but when we are together, she focuses her attention on me. She asks about what is going on in my life, she laughs with me. I feel welcomed and loved and a part of her life. We are in relationship. When we are not sitting and talking, when we are physically apart, when I think of her, I smile.

I believe that is what God's graciousness is about. When I "get together" with God through prayer, through meditation, through keeping him in my thoughts, I am in relationship with him. I am aware of his gentleness, his love, his warmth, his understanding, his laughter.

When are you aware of the graciousness of God in your life?

Tuesday • Rosie would give me anything I ask for that she has the power to give. I know that. I know that I could go to her for anything. At one point a number of years ago, I was struggling with a momentous decision in my life. I could tell Rosie was not totally onboard with the way I was leaning in this decision, but she listened and enveloped me in a loving hug. In the years since I made that decision, she has not once criticized me or been judgmental. She has graciously accepted my decision and supports me in its consequences. There is always a loving hug.

God graciously accepts our decisions even when they are not ones he supports. He graciously gave us a free will. Even if our decisions and behaviors are not in keeping with God's love, he supports us as we live the consequences.

Do you feel God's gracious acceptance even when you make decisions that are not in keeping with his love? If friends can accept and understand us, how much greater is God's acceptance and understanding? We often don't give God credit for being God!

Wednesday • When our decisions and the subsequent behaviors get us in a heap of trouble or create stress in our lives, it is essential that we remember God is present. He is present here, just as he was present at the wedding feast. He is not only present, but he is ready to help. Rosie could not give me anything to fix the stress created by my decision, but she was present every step of the way. When I would say at the beginning of a phone call, "Rosie, I'm so sorry to bother you with this again, but I just need to talk," she would say, "Penny, I am here for you no matter what."

That is what Christ says to us. "I am here for you no matter what." Scripture tells us we don't bother him with our requests. "He is more ready to give than we are to ask."

It can feel like we ask Christ over and over for help, and we think it's possible he grows tired of our petitions. His word promises that he is present here with us and that he will give us strength and courage.

Do you worry that you "bother" Christ with your many petitions? At times do they seem too trivial and at times insurmountable? Do you remember that he promises to be present with you?

Thursday • In my work with women addicted to alcohol and drugs, they often have been "trying" to get clean and sober for years. Their stories are often sad and desperate. They try and try on their own, with little or no success. They feel guilty, ashamed, and hopeless. They even pray. One woman said, "I prayed for so long that God would send me an angel." On the first anniversary of her recovery, she said, "I didn't believe that I could do this. I tried and tried so many times. It was not until I learned about putting my recovery in my relationship with God and began to have a little hope that things began to change. I really believe God sent an angel who opened me to a new way of thinking about my recovery and pushed me into doing things differently. I stopped trying and began doing."

For those with other areas of their lives to change, it is about stopping the *trying* and beginning the *doing*. It's about paying attention to the people God places in our lives who can lead to new ways of approaching an issue or behavior. It's about following the leads of people who can show us new ways of being with those we love, new ways of dealing with our anger, new ways of working through long-held resentments. We stop trying and begin risking new behaviors. God places those "angels" in our lives for a purpose.

What area of your life would you like to change? Have you been trying? What would it take to move you from "trying" to "doing"? Who in your life can lead you toward that change?

Friday • When we try and try and nothing changes, it feels hopeless and we feel helpless. Self-help groups have a saying, "If nothing changes, nothing changes." What needs to change? Several changes may need to occur, and one may be that we think we have control...that we can do it all ourselves.

Many of us grew up in chaotic homes where we felt we had to be in control. Even now, when there is a stressful situation, we feel the need to take charge, to be in control. But there are many situations in which we have no control—even if we know the situation is impacting us or those we love.

Part of what needs to change is to accept that Christ is with us. Through his graciousness we are molded and formed by all of our experiences...even the messes we create by thinking we have control. If we let him, Christ will mold us. We are the clay, he is the potter. He is with us in all of the messiness of our lives.

Can you pray to let go of the need for control and accept his gracious presence?

Saturday • How can we bring a sense of God with us in our lives? How can we remind ourselves that we are not in control? Signs are there when we are open to recognizing them. In self-help recovery groups, people are reminded of their recovery by having a chip or coin in their pocket. I recall a very popular movie in which there was a scene in the emergency room of a hospital. The movie had no religious theme, but right there on the wall was a crucifix...a sign, a reminder. It caught my attention. What was it saying?

At Christmas each year we sing the hymn "O Come, O Come, Emmanuel." In this hymn we pray that Christ comes to this world. We should be singing this hymn all year. Emmanuel means "God with us." His gracious love is here.

Is he with you today? What is your reminder?

Week 6: Freedom

Jesus did this, the first of his signs, in Cana of Galilee, and revealed his glory: and his disciples believed in him. –JOHN 2:11

Sunday • When Jesus turned water into wine at Cana, it was a sign of what he wants to do with our lives. He wants to make us new. He wants to give us a life of quality. He wants to transform us. And what does that life look like? How might it be described? What is its primary characteristic? Freedom.

He frees us to love instead of being selfish. He frees us to care instead of being self-seeking. He frees us to take risks for his sake instead of always playing it safe. He frees us to laugh at ourselves instead of wallowing in guilt and shame. He frees us to dance the dance of joy and excitement instead of burying our heads in gloom. He frees us to be free.

And coupled with that, he frees us to live a life of servanthood. We are free to serve those who hurt and struggle and cry and despair. He frees us to reach out to the poor and hungry and addicted. He frees us to be sensitive to the needs of our spouse, our children, our neighbors, and our fellow workers.

John tells us that the wine Jesus produces was substantially better than the wine that had first been served. The life Christ offers you is greater in quality than any life you could put together for yourself. And he gives it to you as a free gift. Take and drink of it. It's the best life you could ever have!

Monday • The freedom we experience in early recovery from addiction or the freedom we feel when any burden is removed is a freedom "from"—a freedom from guilt, or maybe a freedom from a debt. People burn their mortgage book when they pay their last mortgage payment—accompanied with laughter and smiles. Graduates throw their graduation hats in the air with joy and excitement—freedom from classes and homework and stress. Rarely do they know what they are moving "to." That's part of the excitement and also part of the fear.

We move "from" and into "to" when we begin to experience the transformation of our lives through Christ's gracious love. We move from lives of burden and remorse or guilt and shame to lives of freedom.

Rarely do we know what lies ahead for us. Rarely do we take time to consider what difference this new awareness of Christ in our lives might make. We see other people who have moved into a closer relationship with God and we envy their peace. They walk with a lighter step. They smile with gentleness. They dance and sing. They are free.

What would a transformed life look like for you—a life based in living Christ's grace?

Tuesday • Being free means being free to take risks. We are free to do things differently in our lives. We are free to be different people. Those risks can be big or small.

Two exemplary people in my life come to mind as wonderful models of freedom to live their lives in Christ. One is a woman, Rita, who has spent her professional life developing residential homes for persons being released from prison. The model she developed has been used in several locations in Vermont and followed as a model nationwide. She took a risk to give a new life to people most in need. She met with many challenges, such as "not in my backyard," as well as financial and political roadblocks. In her professional and gentle way she gathered support and proved the viability of these homes. Along the way she developed a volunteer program that brought others into the residential homes to provide meals and conversation to the residents. She brought a new freedom, a transformation, to residents and volunteers alike.

Another friend started a middle school in a troubled neighborhood of a southern city. On a budgetary shoestring he opened a school for young people most at risk for dropping out of high school. The goal is to prepare them scholastically, personally, and spiritually for the challenges of their further education and for life. A recent letter from Mike described the success they have had so far. It also described the primary goal of providing safety for these at-risk children in an environment of responsibility, challenge, success, and knowing God's love. This school, too, has built a strong volunteer program in which children can experience loving consistency that is often missing from their home environments.

Both of these endeavors started as risks. Neither had a guarantee of success. People who had lives based on a strong belief in God started both. Their faith promised that their lives had meaning. The freedom they experienced in that faith must be shared. Both projects are spiritually faith-based. The message of trust in the promises of God is present in the hope and freedom in these places.

Could a new awareness of your transformed life include a willingness to risk involvement in a volunteer project for someone in need?

Wednesday • This new freedom in a life transformed by the miracle of God's grace is also involved in our smaller risks. We can't all start homes for newly released prisoners or schools for children at risk, but we can all look at our own lives and consider risks we can take…risks that will take us into closer relationship with God and with one another. One such risk can be volunteerism with people in need. Another is to examine the attitudes and angers and resentments we hold on to.

I tend to have a very long fuse in circumstances of anger. It takes a lot to get me angry. But once I cross that line, once the fuse reaches the dynamite, I explode. And it's very difficult for me to put the explosive back into the firecracker. I hold on to the anger and resentment, and it's all over the place. This does not make for freedom and peace—in my house or in my soul!

Many of us raised in chaotic homes seem to have this issue of holding on to anger and resentments. When we think of our past we think we have moved on, only to find that a situation similar to one from our past sets off the firecracker. The anger and resentments keep getting re-created. Even when we are with siblings and other family members, we rehearse the old pain, and if we are honest with ourselves, we find we hold on to it almost like a security blanket. In part, the old pain defines who we are.

That is not freedom! The old pain is what Christ wants to transform in our lives. He promises that if we are open to his grace, he will move us to genuine forgiveness—forgiveness of our own sins and our forgiveness of others.

What would your life feel like if you could let go of the old anger and resentments? What would that new freedom be like?

Thursday • Another way to use this new freedom that comes with transformation of our lives came to my attention recently. A young professional woman said that she has lost her "filter." She says she is so burned out in her current position that she tends to say whatever comes to mind. She indicated this could result in her saying things in a nonproductive or even hurtful way. She used to be able to hear a statement in her head before she spurted it out and was able to modify it if necessary.

She realizes she still has the capability to "filter" and needs to take the time to do that. In other words, she has the ability to say things in a grace-filled manner that people will hear as supportive. She can do that without losing the point she wants to make. Her fatigue and frustration do not need to have control. She has the freedom to think through who and how she wants to be.

Is there an area in your life in which it would be helpful to reinstate your "filter"? What are the clues?

Friday • This new freedom moves us to dance and sing, and it also leads us to servanthood. Rita and Mike have both been recognized in their communities for their contributions to others, but neither is personally comfortable with those dinners and awards. They accept the recognition because it brings more awareness of the projects themselves.

Servanthood in our lives means our experiences on a daily level. It means a daily recognition of ways to experience Christ's love of us and to share that love with others. We are free to live our lives in an extraordinary way says theologian Dietrich Bonhoeffer. That extraordinary way can be one of monumental tasks or one of quiet involvement. Rita and Mike spend each extraordinary day in their organizations living Christ's promises of freedom and hope in servanthood with the prisoners, students, workers, teachers, and volunteers.

Do you spend each extraordinary day in servanthood with your parents, spouses, children, coworkers, and fellow commuters?

Saturday • A friend with her first year of recovery from alcoholism loves the freedom she has...the freedom from the guilt, shame, and hopelessness of the disease. She is amazed that even the thought of drinking has been removed from her daily struggle. When the thought does return, she finds herself thinking she does not want to go back to all of that. She fears even one drink would escalate over time to the old patterns. She believes in the miracle of transformation of her life.

The transformation of our lives that God offers is in servanthood to those in need. Sometimes the person most in need is myself.

What transformation in your life would lead to freedom... freedom in Christ's gracious love?

Week 7: God's Extravagance

Now standing there were six stone water jars for the Jewish rites of purification, each holding twenty or thirty gallons.–JOHN 2:6

Sunday • When my husband was a kid, he loved to play basketball. He asked his dad if he would put up a basketball hoop on the front of the garage. Instead, his dad paved a portion of the backyard with green asphalt and attached a new metal backboard and rim. To say the least, what his dad did was absolutely extravagant. It is one of my husband's most treasured childhood memories.

Extravagance also marked the Cana wedding. The thing to take special note of is the amount of wine Jesus produced. It was six stone jars. In today's way of measurements, that would be between 120 and 180 gallons of wine. Remember, this was after the first serving of wine had run out.

This sign points to the incredible generosity of God. It demonstrates his amazing extravagance. Some people act as though God is stingy. They think of God as someone whose hand must be pried open before he will pour out his good gifts. Some think we have to make a deal with God, we have to bargain with him before he will give.

But God doesn't expect nor ask that. He is much more ready to give than we are to ask. He lavishes gifts upon us. He pours out. He gives and keeps on giving. Look at the cross if you want proof of God's overflowing generosity. He loves us so much that he gives up his own Son...for *us*.

Monday • My husband remembers helping with the digging and leveling necessary to transform that backyard. He had only requested a hoop be attached to the garage, but his dad wanted him to have the best possible practice area.

Sometimes we also ask for only the first part of a change in our lives from God. We ask God to take away the addiction or the habit that is creating stress in our lives. When we ask God to keep us from buying the drug or buying the expensive item we cannot afford or eating the extra doughnuts or ice cream, we are only asking for the first part of the transformation. But God is generous beyond measure. He wants to give us the best. He wants our whole lives to be transformed, and he wants us to be involved in that transformation.

What have you asked God for in an effort to change some part of your life? Have you risked thinking and asking for transformation that would change your relationship with God—your whole life? How involved are you willing to be?

Tuesday • The amount of water Christ changed into wine is truly amazing. Those of us challenged by alcoholism cringe at thoughts of that quantity being available. But rather than thinking of that quantity as a trigger, it is useful to think of it as representative of God's gracious, abundant, generous, extravagant love. Or think of those jars as filled with hope…hope that regardless of our struggles, our challenges, our anxieties, or our addictions, God's love will never run out. Even when we return to our old behavior that led us into trouble, God's generous love and forgiveness are always there. We never need to be afraid to return to God and ask him to be with us.

A small framed note from his dad hangs in my husband's study. It says, "Show them what you've got, son." His dad wrote it the night before a big game. That is what God says to us even when we might not be having our best "season." He's not there to belittle us if we miss a "shot." He's not there to criticize our style. God is there to encourage us, to be in relationship with us. He wants to be with us to "show them what we've got." His quantity of love and grace and forgiveness never runs out.

What "note" do you have from God that reminds you of his extravagant quantities of hope, love, grace, and forgiveness? How can you show yourself "what you've got"—with God's help?

Wednesday • All of us can have doubts and questions about this idea of God's generosity. We see poverty, loss of jobs, loss of homes, even illness and abuse, and it all seems so unfair and even evil. Sometimes the world is unfair and evil. We question, Where is God in all of this? Where is God's love and grace?

When we have times of doubt and questions, it helps to remember it is not God who is stingy or who creates evil; it is the world that creates the unfairness and evil. It is the world that creates our anxieties. It is our openness to a relationship with God that leads us "away from temptation and delivers us from evil."

When it seems like the jars of grace and forgiveness are running low in our lives, when the unfairness and evil of the world seem to have the upper hand, that is the time to pray for an openness to God's presence in our lives. It takes a daily, sometimes an hourly, and sometimes a minute-by-minute visitation with Christ to be reminded that his generous, abundant grace will be with us through this.

Do you sometimes rail at God for the unfairness and evil in the world and all around you? Do you stop and remember to ask him to be with you during those times?

Thursday • When life has been particularly challenging, it can be difficult to see any transformation taking place. It can be difficult to see God's presence. A woman in a Bible class talked of her estrangement from God when she was first diagnosed with lupus. She was confined to a wheelchair and considered giving up—resigning herself to a life of immobility. She was angry at the world and at God. "I was young; my life was over." But little by little, she "felt a tap on my shoulder. It was like God was saying, 'Come on. We can do something about this.'" She said, "My mother is real feisty, and she challenged me and urged me not to give up. So with the help of God and my mother and my own hardheadedness, I learned to walk again." This woman talks of the transformation in her life, not as the miracle of Christ telling the man to "get up and walk," but as the slow transformation of her new openness to God in her life. That new openness and relationship gave her hope and the courage to be with God as he worked his miracle.

God's transformation of our lives is not magic. It is the slow awareness of his generosity, abundant love, and forgiveness. Are you aware of this transformation?

Friday • Every day Christ lavishes his extravagant grace and love on us. We sense it in the change of seasons, the stars on a cold winter's night, the warmth of the sun. We must stop and take time to see and acknowledge this generous God. And we feel it in the smaller personal miracles. My younger son recently received a promotion that he had been told he would not receive. A few years earlier he had been devastated when told his career had hit a roadblock—especially since he had been on the "fast track" for several years. But now with this promotion, all of that was past. The joy in his voice when he told me of the promotion was a song in my heart. It was not the promotion that pleased me so much but the joy in my son's voice. It was an awareness of God's graciousness.

We are often so busy, so consumed by our worldliness, that we miss the evidence of God's lavish goodness in our lives.

Where is the evidence of God's extravagant, lavish goodness in your world today? Where have you heard the joy?

Saturday • The joy in my son's voice and the joy I felt in my heart at his news is one of God's beautiful mysteries. Another beautiful mystery is the joy one begins to feel in early recovery from addiction or any struggle. We feel a freedom, a release from bondage. It is the beginning of a new life. This joy is a gracious gift from a gracious God. It is the result of God's lavish extravagance. It is not something we have done or something we have earned. He has transformed our fears into possibility.

Do you thank God over and over for this gift of recovery—recovery from any demon? Are you in awe of the mystery of his extravagant love for you?

Week 8: God's Abundant Love

Jesus did this, the first of his signs, in Cana of Galilee, and revealed his glory; and his disciples believed in him.–JOHN 2:11

Sunday • Christ produced fifty cases of wine at the wedding feast in Cana. Our God is not only good; he is unbelievably generous. By any standard measurement, he is extravagant. There is no limit to God's love.

The sad thing is that often we don't take advantage of God's generosity. It would be like my putting a million dollars in your bank account—a free gift with no strings attached—and you fail to use the money. As a result, you lead an impoverished life.

We often do that sort of thing in our daily lives. We struggle with our problems, our difficulties, our addictions, and never bother to share these burdens with the Father. We hang on to the weight of our guilt and shame and never take the free gift of forgiveness that comes from the crucified and risen Christ.

However, there is no need to live our lives as though they were wedding receptions where the wine has run out. There is a superabundance of the grace of God; no need of ours could ever exhaust it. It makes no difference what life has been up to this point; the love of Christ is more than enough for you. It is there for you. Open your heart and your life to him and discover for yourself how generous and extravagant God is. He is waiting to be for you what he claims to be.

Monday • Yesterday's reading compared God's generosity to having a free gift of a million dollars in a bank account. If we never used that money and led an impoverished life, people would wonder about our sanity. On the other hand, we have also heard stories of people who won millions of dollars in the lottery and squandered the money. Their lives were changed dramatically, and they had no plan for their new lives. Their lives ultimately turned out worse than before.

The winning of the lottery can also be a way to think of the extravagant generosity of God. Once we open ourselves to God's generosity, our lives are changed dramatically. But we'd better think through what that means for us. We'd better have a plan as to how to use God's never-ending gift of love.

Do you have a thought of how your life might change when you begin to understand God's extravagant gift of love? Any plan?

Tuesday • Before we devise a plan for this new life lived in forgiveness and love, we must work on being open to the gift. People who play the lottery believe they have a chance to win. We need to begin to be open to the reality we have already won—God's forgiveness. We need to be open to the "prize" out there—God's love. If we want to receive this gift of life lived in forgiveness and love, we at least need to "buy a ticket."

So often in our anxieties, our difficulties, our addictions, we are closed to the idea that a prize exists. We have so often promised ourselves that we will change our behavior or our thinking, and so often we return to the old destructive patterns. We are discouraged; we won't even buy a ticket for a chance at change. We are closed. Our guilt and shame from our past failures shut us down.

But then one day we see a sign to buy a ticket, just to have some hope. The sign might be in the example of someone else or maybe in the memory of a time when life was easier or maybe in a whispered prayer we hardly even know we utter. And we begin to pay attention. We begin to recognize the prize is there, just waiting for us. We begin to be willing to take the chance, to be open, to buy a ticket—to have hope, to pray for an awareness of this gift of extravagant love and forgiveness.

Are you open to the idea that there is a prize and you have already won?

Wednesday • You have already won! Christ has already given you the prize. He has done this with his life, death, and resurrection. You simply need to begin to bring that belief into your life. And sometimes that is a very difficult thing to do. It can be difficult to remember daily that God is with you in every part of your struggle and challenge. It is difficult to remember daily that God is with you in the joys and successes. He is in the courage to make those daily decisions that lead you into recovery and peace.

And it can be difficult to remember that he forgives all our sins of the past...a very real prize. Sometimes family members and others are happy to remind us of those sins and the ways we have failed them. Sometimes they do that in subtle, passive ways, and sometimes they do that in angry, aggressive ways. A friend tells how her adult children "laugh" at her past failures when they are together. Her daughter never fails to tell her of their reminiscences. God never laughs at her failures. He holds her in his forgiveness. God says, "I remember your sins no more."

Can you begin to let go of the guilt and shame? Can you begin to be open to God's love and forgiveness? The prize!

Thursday • People who lived through the Great Depression and those who have lost much in the recent recession often create new patterns of saving. They are reluctant to spend and don't believe there is enough money to meet their needs. My mother was a child of the Depression and had great difficulty spending money even when the economy improved. Much of her conversation centered around what was in her savings account and whether it would last through her later years. She kept track of every check she ever wrote!

This bank account of God's love and forgiveness is not like that. It is replenished every time we look into it. God wants us to use this gift. He wants us to look into this account by being in relationship with him. He wants us to talk with him. He wants us to unburden ourselves to him. He wants us to draw on his forgiveness by confessing our sins. He wants us to participate in the Eucharist and know the peace that surpasses all understanding.

Today can you look into God's gift of forgiveness and love and feel the peace?

Friday • When my daughter was about three years old, color television was new. We did not have one, but my parents did. The first time that television was on at their house, she delightedly exclaimed, "The Flintstones are in color!" She then turned to her adoring grandfather and asked, "Can you get my mommy one of those TVs?" And, of course, the next Christmas "Santa" brought a new color television to our house.

Loving fathers and grandfathers do that. They give without

question. All we need to do is ask. And it helps if we ask with delight and with belief that they will provide.

Do you believe your heavenly Father can and will provide? Do you believe he wants to be all that he claims to be, just for you?

Saturday • Who does God claim to be?

Our Redeemer—Daily he forgives our sins.

Our Creator—Daily he renews his life in us.

Our Savior—Daily he saves us from ourselves.

Our Deliverer—Daily he saves us from the evil around us.

Our Father—Daily he holds us, comforts us, and disciplines us.

Our Friend—Daily he listens and is by our side.

He is all of these things. In what ways are you open to God's power in all of these promises?

Lent: Blessings Showered Upon Us Through Jesus

During the season of Lent we use chapter 8 of the Letter of Saint Paul to the Romans as the basis for Sunday devotions and daily meditations. Why Romans 8? Because it so clearly states the blessings that God showers upon us through the life, death, and resurrection of Jesus Christ.

Week 9: No Condemnation

There is therefore now no condemnation for those who are in Christ Jesus.–ROMANS 8:1

Sunday • Fear of condemnation is an issue many of us struggle with for a large part of our lives. We also often condemn others when we fail to measure up in our marriage, in our job, with our children. And self-condemnation hangs over us like a dark cloud. But by far, we most fear condemnation by a holy God who is justly angered by our failures and shortcomings. And no matter how hard we try to make amends, no matter how hard we try to make atonement, we always seem to come up short.

We received ashes on our foreheads on Ash Wednesday and were reminded once again of our mortality and our brazen sinfulness. The ashes are enough to make us hide our heads in despair except for one thing: *The ashes placed on our foreheads are in the shape of a cross.* That means there is no condemnation for all who belong to Jesus Christ. He took our condemnation upon himself so that we might be holy and blameless before God—now and at the last day. He has taken us off death row and given us a new life.

Monday • The word *condemned*, or *condemnation*, has such a sense of darkness and finality. The dictionary's definition of the word offers a sense of strong disapproval or being held guilty. Then reading the definition further, we see a reference to being destined for an unhappy fate or being declared unfit for use. Strong words! Many of us carry around this sense of strong disapproval. We feel we're destined for an unhappy fate, and it colors our general feelings about life. Nevertheless, we put on a happy face. We go about our business and tasks, presenting to the world a mask of having it all together, or at least looking as if we're satisfied with our life.

But underneath that mask, we know that in many ways we are not living up to the life and purpose God has in mind for us. We know we're faking it, and we condemn ourselves for that. We know part of what we present to the world is a fraud. It's hard to "put on a happy face" when what we're feeling is "an unhappy fate."

The wonderful news is we can take off our masks. God loves us just as we are. In what areas of your life do you feel like a fraud? Today can you ask God to help you give yourself a little slack, to remove that mask?

Tuesday • The feeling of being condemned, of strong disapproval, gets etched into our being very early in our lives. Well-meaning parents and teachers criticize our exuberant, natural, childlike behavior, and we wind up feeling we've done something very wrong. We grow up believing we're "bad." As adults, "bad" turns into not keeping up. Keeping up in society and culture places demands on us to earn lots of money, to have perfect children, to be thin, to dress like a model, or to have perfect abs. We tell ourselves we must be perfect spouses and "be happy."

We know we are not perfect, and we know the picture we present to the world is not who we really are. These condemnations and criticisms from the world and from ourselves are not the messages we need to listen to.

Christ has a different message for us.

Can you begin to hear the false values of the messages of reproach from society and culture? Can you replace those condemnations with the message that you "are in Christ Jesus"?

Wednesday • We live in self-reproach. It's a constant murmur in our heads and in our hearts. A friend's husband recently died. She cannot let go of the fact that he demanded she take him home from the hospital to die. Instead, he was moved to a hospice where he could receive the frequent treatments he needed to remove the fluid from his lungs. Without those treatments he struggled to breathe and his death at home might well have been traumatic. This loving wife cannot let go of the fact that she "did not get him home." She felt she had not "done enough." When any of us feel that way, we're apt to sink into guilt and self-condemnation. We hold ourselves to an unrealistic standard of perfection.

What standard does our loving God hold us to? The only one he asks of us is to "do the loving thing." Is there a situation in your life that you've been feeling guilty about? You might have handled it differently, but it was also the best you could do at the time. Is there something you can do today to be more loving to someone involved in that situation?

Thursday • It can be very difficult to take into our head and heart the real understanding and belief that we are forgiven—that Christ really has paid the ransom for our sins. If we have hurt others by our addictions, by our anger, by our self-centeredness, we can apologize over and over, but it often doesn't feel like enough. We can't take back the words. We can't make up for the broken promises. We can't make up the time we lost with them.

Guilt is not always a bad thing. It is a reminder that we have not been living the life God wishes for us. The guilt helps us avoid slipping back into the old patterns. But if the guilt and condemnation keep us living under a dark cloud, that is not the life God wishes for us either.

God wants us to know at some deep level that we are forgiven. That "knowing" is not a scientific knowledge, but a deep sense of being held in God's loving arms.

When you struggle with feelings of guilt, can you move through prayer into God's loving arms?

Friday • If you were raised in a tradition that distributed ashes on Ash Wednesday, as a child you might have had a sense of the ritual as something austere and ominous. What are these gray smudges? But then you were taught that the ashes are a symbol of your faith, and you wore them because they identified you as a Christian.

Unfortunately, what was often missing in that smear of gray was the very important fact that the ashes are placed on your forehead in the form of a cross. As adults, it is vital that we receive the ashes with a firm awareness that this marking of the cross tells us that God holds us blameless. Christ took our sins upon himself. He erases those sins from us, today and every day, until we die.

Today we get to live a life free from condemnation—free from guilt, free from self-reproach, free from the dark cloud.

Given that you are now free from condemnation, free from your sins, how will you live your life differently?

Saturday • Remember the movie *The Green Mile*? Sadly in our society, many prisoners live for years and years on death row. They live in isolation, cut off from family, restricted in movement or from any semblance of a normal life. In recent years, some of those people condemned to die have been found innocent through DNA testing. One can only imagine the joy and excitement they must feel as they step out of those prison clothes and into their new freedom.

We have been given that new freedom from death row by the birth, life, death, and resurrection of Jesus Christ. We have been given his new life.

Do you experience the joy and excitement of that new life? Have you stepped out from the prison of condemnation?

Week 10: No Fear

For you did not receive a spirit of slavery to fall back into fear, but you have received a spirit of adoption....We cry, "Abba! Father!"

–ROMANS 8:15

Sunday • What fears haunt your life and occupy your dreams at night? The fear of failure? The fear of disapproval? The fear of criticism? The fear of death? It's amazing how fear can shape our behavior and attitudes. For example, we often won't take risks because we're afraid of failure, or we frequently don't speak up because we fear disapproval.

Saint Paul says we are no longer slaves to fear; we no longer need to revolve our lives around fear. We are free to walk out into the sunshine of God's gift of freedom. Why? Because in Jesus Christ, God became our Father who protects us, shields us, and guards over us. God has established such a close and intimate relationship with us through Jesus' life, death, and resurrection that he invites us to call him "Abba, Father" and to share all our fears with him.

Monday • Our 24-7 news focuses on all things traumatic and fearful—wars, murders, violence, drugs, financial collapse.

Politics and feuding political parties predict dire consequences if we elect the opposition. The most popular video games are about death and violence and how powerful it feels to be the person doing the killing.

No wonder we go through our days tense and anxious. And then the medical community offers us pills to "fix" our nervous anxieties. But no amount of medication can erase the damaging, self-perpetuating fear that we don't live up to the picture we project to the outside world. People may discover we are a fraud; we don't have it all together. We live in the fear that others will come to know our insecurities and our vulnerabilities.

Saint Paul assures us that Christ does not want us to live in fear. We are not to be a slave to fear. We have received a spirit that saves us from living in fear.

Notice what news stories send shivers of anxiety or fear through you. Is that what God wants you to focus on as part of your life as his beloved son or daughter?

Tuesday • When I was a student in a counseling course, the teacher had us work in pairs for a particular exercise. As part of the exercise he gave us the beginning phrase of a sentence, and we were to complete it out loud immediately to our partner. A phrase that helped lead me out of my fear was, "If you really knew me…"; I completed the phrase, "…you wouldn't like me." That response told me I was in trouble.

I was struggling mightily with my alcoholism at the time, but I was putting on the face of devoted wife, mother, nurse, and so on and so on. I had been fooling myself and my loved ones, and ultimately undermining my spirituality. I was living in fear that someone would find out I wasn't this pillar of the community, that I was really a sneak and a liar. Through my awareness and prayer, I learned to make changes that led me out of my fear.

That exercise occurred on the Tuesday night before Ash

Wednesday. On Ash Wednesday I shared this new awareness with my priest and began my journey out of fear. Yes, I believe in miracles!

"If you really knew me..." How would you complete this phrase? Would it make any difference in your life?

Wednesday • Bailey, our adopted Labrador retriever, is an absolute delight when we are at home quietly living our lives. But when I take her for a walk on our quiet mountain road, her behavior becomes unpredictable. Off leash, she frolics in the woods, chases chipmunks, and jumps in every pond and stream... the picture of joy. However, when another dog approaches too closely, she turns incredibly hostile. She barks and growls and acts very ferocious. I wonder what happened in her past that provokes this? What is she afraid of?

Things have happened to each of us in the past as well. Those experiences often determine how we interact with people and what we are afraid of. My husband and I may never know what happened to Bailey that makes her act so ferociously, but it is important for us to think about what has happened to us in the past that makes us so afraid.

As you go through today, consider the things you fear. Are you afraid someone will criticize you? What does that do to your behavior or interaction with them? Smile at your new awareness, and ask God to put his arm around you as you respond differently.

Thursday • I was e-mailing a friend some words of spiritual encouragement and said, "I don't want you to think I've become a spiritual nut but..." and then I proceeded to type a biblical quotation. What made me embarrassed to quote Scripture to her? What made me think I had to apologize before sharing God's words? What made me afraid to share my faith that this verse from Scripture would bring her some support and healing? What societal or cultural value took precedent over what I truly believe? I felt guilty at my hesitancy, but it certainly got my attention!

Are you also reluctant to mention your faith? Why?

Friday • Last week we mentioned the joy and excitement that a prisoner found innocent must feel when released from death row—even from prison. After years behind bars, he or she will find the world changed dramatically. Anyone would need time to assimilate and adjust to that new life. When we begin to realize that Christ's taking on our sins released us from prison, what do we feel? Does the joy of living our lives in this new reality begin to enter our souls?

When we reenter a world changed by our awareness of forgiveness, an awareness that we no longer have to be "slaves to fear," can we begin to take risks, speak up, and change our behavior? How? How today?

Saturday • We are filled with anxiety if we are a slave to fear. But how do we move beyond it? How do we begin to change our behavior so we don't constantly have to be afraid? Saint Paul suggests we view God as a Father. That seems like a wonderful, gentle way to begin. Just as the prisoner stepping out to a new world and a new freedom takes hesitant steps and must adjust slowly to the new world, we, too, begin slowly with this new world of forgiveness. Each morning we whisper, "Abba, Father." We take time to remember that God has given us a new spirit, a spirit that removes our fear, removes the cloud of darkness, removes the tension that makes us respond in less than loving ways.

We pray. We go to the Eucharist. We receive the Spirit that reminds us that God is with us always. He gives us strength.

When you think of God as Father, whom do you see?

Week 11: Children of God

...it is that very Spirit bearing witness with our spirit that we are children of God, and if children, then heirs, heirs of God and joint heirs with Christ—if, in fact, we suffer with him so that we may also be glorified with him. –ROMANS 8:16–17

Sunday • Sometimes it feels as if everyone is trying to define who we are. Our spouse describes us one way; our children another; and our friends describe us in yet another way. It's no wonder we are frequently confused about our identity—so much so that if someone asks us, "Who are you?" we fumble around trying to come up with a precise answer.

But it's not necessary to fumble and hesitate. God has given us his Spirit, who testifies that we are God's children. We are God's children. God is our Father. We *know* who we are.

And we're not just "anybody," we're royalty. Saint Paul says we are heirs of God the king and coheirs with our brother, Christ. Imagine that! We have unlimited treasures awaiting us. Of course we may suffer; anyone who is identified as a follower of Christ is going to suffer rejection, ridicule, and disapproval from the world. Christ died and so will we. But it's worth it; just consider what awaits us!

Monday • These are interesting questions: How do my friends define or identify me? How do my children describe me? How does my spouse identify me? What words do I use to describe myself?

Recently we went through a receiving line composed of persons of varying ages. We did not know most of the people at the event. One young woman was dressed in a very uptown style, certainly more stylish than we normally see in our rural Vermont town. My husband leaned in to speak to her and said,

"You look like you must be from New York." She tossed her head back in delighted laughter and said to the person next to her, "He nailed it. He said I must be from New York."

Our style of dress identifies us. Our vocabulary identifies us. How we carry our bodies tells a lot about who we think we are.

Today, ask a spouse or friend how they would describe you. Do they mention anything that identifies your belief that you are a child of God?

Tuesday • As we "mature," my husband and I tend to prefer small gatherings of friends rather than large social events. Of course a large party can be fun and can inspire interesting introductions and stimulating conversations. But in small parties there is more opportunity to get to know people's stories. And we all have stories—incidents that have formed who we are at our core. In smaller gatherings it seems there is more chance we actually will hear those stories and get to know the person's challenges, successes, and beliefs.

Do your friends ever tell you stories of their own faith...the stories that formed who they are? Do you tell yours to them? What would those stories be?

Do you believe you are a child of God? How would that be reflected in your life as others see you?

Wednesday • Saint Paul uses the phrase, "The very Spirit bearing witness with our spirit that we are children of God." *Bearing witness* are strong words. They sound very legalese. It seems to fit in with some of the words we've already been discussing: *condemnation* and *slave*. *Witness* conjures up images of a courtroom and swearing on a Bible that what we say is true.

Not long ago I had to testify in a murder case. It was a stressful situation. What I had written in the police report at the time of the incident was questioned by the defense. I felt accused and challenged. He made what I knew to be true sound weak.

When the evil in the world makes us question if we are God's children, we need to remember that the "Spirit with our spirit" bears witness that we are. What we know to be true is not weak.

This is a promise of God! We are God's children. This is part of the "legal" covenant God makes with us. It is true. It is strong. We don't need to question it.

Thursday • The knowledge or understanding that we are children of God gives us a sense of security. That feeling of security helps us move out of our fears into a sense of being held in safety. An image of a loving parent paints a picture of someone who is always available—who provides food, shelter, and clothing as we're growing up, quickly responds to our phone calls and texts. He or she takes an interest in our lives yet sets limits so we can find our own way. Sometimes that is not the person who actually parented us, but it's the image we have of an ideal parent.

When God promises that we are his children, when the Spirit bears witness to that promise, we can picture that loving Father as present in our lives, walking with us in our challenges.

Do you picture an image of God when you think of him or pray to him? Where did the image come from? Is it an image that gives you peace and rest?

Friday • If you have inherited money or property from someone's estate, you know that can sometimes be a mixed blessing. You'll be in the company of lawyers and accountants; you'll deal with insurance and taxes and co-heirs' fights. Relationships become strained over money, and families often fight over the will or the division of material goods.

Saint Paul's Scripture passage calls us "heirs" and "joint heirs" with Christ. Heirs and joint heirs of what? Heirs of God's kingdom. A whole kingdom awaits us as we recognize ourselves as children of God.

And what does that kingdom consist of? Certainly not gold and jewels, but forgiveness and grace. That kingdom does not await us in the sky, but right here on this earth on this very day. When we recognize that we are children of God, we recognize ourselves as forgiven and blessed. As people who are forgiven and blessed, we are free to take that inheritance and share it with others.

How? How today?

Saturday • Ways in which we share our inheritance of forgiveness and grace may, in fact, cause us to experience rejection, ridicule, and disapproval. When we act in ways that demonstrate forgiveness and grace, current society may laugh or sneer at our behavior. I remember a tragic traffic accident near us in which one car crossed the yellow line and caused a head-on crash, killing a father and his ten-year-old son. The wife was left with a severe brain injury. In the newspaper report, the adult brother of the deceased father said, "I don't blame the other driver. Things happened that were bad for everyone." What an expression of forgiveness and grace! In today's society we would more likely hear, "Call the best lawyer in town!"

Being God's children, having the inheritance of God's kingdom of forgiveness and grace, is an incredible gift. And it's an incredible responsibility to share.

Do you wear the inheritance of forgiveness and grace as a gift to be shared?

Week 12: The Spirit Intercedes

Likewise the Spirit helps us in our weakness; for we do not know how to pray as we ought, but that very Spirit intercedes with sighs too deep for words. And God, who searches the heart, knows what is the mind of the Spirit, because the Spirit intercedes for the saints according to the will of God. –ROMANS 8:26–27

Sunday • This passage from Saint Paul is really good news to those of us who have difficulty with prayer. I'm one of those people. It's not that I think God doesn't hear my prayers or answer them. It's not that I don't recall the prayers I learned as a child. I do. Rather, my struggle with prayer is that sometimes my life becomes so confusing and messy; my problems become so deep and profound that I don't know what to pray. I don't know what I need. I don't know what to say.

That is why Saint Paul's words are so comforting and reassuring. We don't have to find the "right" words. He promises us that the Spirit intercedes for us with sighs that words cannot express. The Spirit takes our problems, our struggles, and our pain that we can't put into words and offers them to the Father, who knows already what we need. You may feel that God doesn't understand because you can't express your problem properly, but God does understand and does respond! That is God's promise.

Monday • "We do not know how to pray as we ought, but that very Spirit intercedes" for us. Two parts of this sentence touch me. First, I notice that Saint Paul does not say what we ought to pray *for.* Way too often it seems my prayers are *for* something… for a promotion, for good weather, for a good report. But prayer is simply to be communication with God, as we would talk to a friend or listen to a loving parent. It is sharing our struggles, our fears, our joys, and our successes.

Second, this Scripture says that that very Spirit intercedes for us. I also find that reassuring. I am embarrassed to admit it, but sometimes I forget that the Spirit is right here, ready to take my thoughts, my needs, and my struggles to God. Even when I can't find the right words, when I feel alone in the mess I have made, the Spirit shapes the words I can't find.

Prayer doesn't have to be formal. I don't have to assume a particular posture, although being on my knees does help me focus. I just need to quiet myself and open my heart. The Spirit is there. Joan Chittister calls this "melting into God."

Take a few minutes today to pray—to talk and listen to God about what is going on in your life. Quiet yourself and know the Spirit will be with you.

Tuesday • Sometimes I just pray, "Help!" It's immediate. Maybe I need patience. Now! Often my tone of voice projects my frustration or impatience, especially with those closest to me. Why do I use that tone, and why is it mostly with family members? I never use that tone with friends or coworkers. So my prayer becomes, "Help me hear this tone before it comes out of my mouth. Help me express this another way—a more loving way."

And it is almost a miracle that when I pray for patience and to be aware of my tone, it happens. I hear it in my head. I make a conscious effort, and the whole atmosphere at home changes. I don't think I'm alone in this. I hear it in supermarkets between parents and children. I hear it between husbands and wives.

Sometimes I just pray what many call the Jesus Prayer: "Lord Jesus Christ, have mercy on me!" One Greek author, Kyriacos Markides, says he prays that over and over, and it's like walking through a polluted city while wearing an oxygen mask over your nose—nothing can touch you.

Prayer helps us call attention to our needs, our shortcomings, and the Spirit intercedes.

What need or shortcoming would you like a little help with today? Can you be open to the Spirit's willingness to help?

Wednesday • "…intercedes with sighs too deep for words."

Sometimes our need is so deep, so painful, that our prayer comes out sounding like a wail. We tearfully groan. At those times, no words can express our deep devastation. We hear that sound at the death of a loved one. It can also come as we experience the devastation we have caused by our addictions, our struggles, and our selfishness. The emptiness, the wound, the longing cannot be put into words. We are at a loss to know how to pray. We are at a loss to even know what we need.

But again Saint Paul assures us that the Spirit is with us and intercedes. The Spirit takes our pain to our loving Father, who hears our wail and cries with us. God takes us in his arms and holds us. We are not alone.

When you feel devastation from a loss or a struggle, can you simply ask the Spirit to help you feel God's loving arms holding you? That is prayer.

Thursday • My favorite psalm, Psalm 139, tells me that God knows what I need before I even ask. "O Lord, you have searched me and known me. You know when I sit down and when I rise up; you discern my thoughts from far away." So why bother to pray? God knows us anyway.

We pray because God wants to be involved in our lives. We pray because communication with God strengthens our relationship with him.

Those of us who are parents know how important talking and listening are in building relationships with our children. As little children and then as teenagers, our children come to us with their needs and wants, cares and concerns. If we want to build strong relationships with them, we listen more than we talk. As teenagers grow into adults, their communication, their willingness to come to us with their cares and concerns, happens less and less. That can be very painful for those of us who still love them dearly. When we are married, the strength of the marriage relationship is built on our willingness to genuinely communicate.

Our relationship with God is built on God's grace and it is strengthened by our willingness to communicate—to listen as well as to talk! That is why we pray even though God already knows our needs.

Can you work toward daily setting aside time to pray—to talk and to listen for God's presence in your life?

Friday • When we pray, when we make time to talk and listen to God, it can seem like a one-way communication. When life is a real mess, when loss has created a pain in our heart, it can feel like we are all alone, that no one is listening, much less God.

But feelings are fickle; they come and go. The friend who is mourning the death of her husband tells me that during some parts of the day, she can go about her business with focus and purpose; at other times she feels abandoned by everyone. People come and go during the day offering support, but as evening comes, she feels no one remembers. That is how the grief process works and that is how we "feel" in our human condition.

Prayer reminds us that we are not abandoned. The Spirit intercedes for us in accordance with God's will. It's not about how we feel. It's about God's promise that he is always with us.

Does your prayer and faith remind you that God is always here with you? Right here! He's promised.

Saturday • Sometimes the things we pray for don't work out: We don't get the job, a person we love betrays us, a health report finds a tumor. But in the long run, our prayers are always heard. They may just not always be heard in the way we expect.

When we are at the point in our lives that we don't have words to pray, when our feelings tell us prayer is useless, that is the time we most urgently need to pray. The prayer we need to remember is the prayer of groaning and listening. In quiet times, our hearts are open. The Spirit is with us and intercedes "in accordance with God's will." He draws us forward.

Today can you pray, "Thy will be done"?

Week 13: The Good

We know that all things work together for good for those who love God.–ROMANS 8:28

Sunday • I am an alcoholic. I do not believe for a moment that it is God's will that I'm an alcoholic, nor do I believe God created me with the disease. So what attitude am I to have toward the disease that has led me to inflict pain on people I love, caused me to jeopardize a career, pushed me into fear and hopelessness, and repeatedly caused me to lie to my family? What good could possibly come out of such a destructive thing?

The answer is "plenty"; plenty good can come out of it if we are open to God's purpose for our lives. Saint Paul says that God is at work for our good in all things, and that includes alcoholism or any other demon, difficulty, or obstacle you may experience in your life. We have a choice. On the one hand, we can become bitter and closed to life, or we can be open to God and ask him to show us what he wants to accomplish in our lives through our struggles and frustration.

What is it going to be? Your choice!

Monday • When I was in post-graduate study at a major Chicago university, I took several advanced biology courses. We studied the human genome and detailed analysis of DNA chromosome structure and function. I would sit in this course absolutely amazed at what science knows and the incredible intricacies of our bodies. It led me to ask one professor, "Do you researchers sit and talk about the connectedness of science and theology? Do you talk about the wonder of God?" I received no response from the professor, but I continued to be in awe of it all.

I was moved enough to start one of my papers with Psalm 139: "It was you who formed my inward parts: you knit me together in my mother's womb. I praise you, for I am fearfully and wonderfully made."

I believe there is a genetic component to this disease of alcoholism, and I also believe "I am fearfully and wonderfully made." Both. It remains an awesome mystery.

Do you struggle with a demon? Are you mystified by what it means in your life? Is there any way this could work for "good"?

Tuesday • When my alcoholism was in its most active period, I would wake up at night in a cold sweat. Then I would walk around the house appalled at my lying, at my anger at those around me, at my inability to control my daily drinking. I would promise myself, "I won't do this tomorrow." But then the next day it would start all over again.

The terror we feel when alcohol or drug use gets out of control identifies this disease as not only a medical condition but also an emotional and a spiritual one. For many of us, the thing that first gets our attention is the trouble we get in...physical trouble, trouble at work, trouble with family, and maybe even trouble with the law. But those things get resolved, one way or another, over time. Away from the alcohol and drugs, our bodies heal. Work and family move forward or change. Even if there is jail time, at some point that is over too. In recovery, life begins to get better.

It is the spiritual dimension of this disease that we need to remember. God is calling us out of this darkness—out of this shame and hopelessness.

What happens to you spiritually when your demon has control? Where is God working in all of this?

Wednesday • Do you believe in miracles? I do. One miracle that has occurred in my life was my alcoholism—not when I bumped into that car in the parking lot, not when a friend saw me drinking out of a vodka bottle. The miracle began to unfold when I began to take a counseling class and was assigned a therapy book. I started reading it in the same room as our liquor cabinet. But I told myself I couldn't drink until I'd read the book, so I'd have to wait a few hours before I could pour one for myself.

A few chapters into the book, my eyes caught a sentence that changed my life. It said, "If there is something in your life you don't like, you can change it." I was stunned. I raised my eyes from the page and looked into a beautiful bright blue sky. *I could change!* I had felt chained to this demon. I felt I had no control. I had felt hopeless. And in one short sentence I heard I could change it.

God's voice comes from surprising places.

Are you open to hearing God's voice? Do you hear God telling you that you can change the destructive part of your life that chains you? Are you listening?

Thursday • Did the change come in one happy day? Of course not. It has been a long process. And though I heard that call to change many years ago, that demon still lurks. It's there more now in the good times—at a celebration or on a vacation or kicking back with friends. A therapist friend says the demon is like a tiger in the grass. We walk along in our new life not paying attention to the tiger, but he is there sneaking along beside us. We might even reach over and try to pet him, thinking he is now tamed. But when we least expect it, that tiger will rise up and bite us "right on the butt." That's the demon of addiction and most other demons.

What can we do? We get help. We call a friend who has the new life. We get rid of the booze and drugs. We find a self-help group. We go. We listen. We read. We get a physical exam. We pray.

What change can you make today that would make a difference in a demon you have? Can you pick up the phone and call a friend? Can you pray? Can you tell God you love him?

Friday • In the middle of a struggle or challenge or addiction, when it feels like the demon has control, it is easy to feel powerless. In fact some self-help groups reinforce this idea of "powerlessness." But what is sometimes missed in that self-help saying is that we are powerless over the disease but not powerless over our lives! We do have choices. They may not be big choices but we do have choices.

Soon after my book *Broken by Addiction, Blessed by God* was published, I was at a church convention and had a table to introduce the book to attendees. A woman I knew slightly from my local parish came up to say hello, and I jokingly encouraged her to buy the book. She did. About a week later she called and asked if she could come by my house. I said yes, and when she came, she asked, "Why did you encourage me to buy your book?" I replied that I was just trying to sell some copies. She smiled and said, "I think it saved my life."

Though my greatest hope is that it might be helpful to people caught in the darkness, I think the miracle is that this woman saw the choices she had. She chose to read the book and then to pick up the phone. She could have made the other choice, "That isn't me…I'm not that bad." She was not powerless. Picking up the phone can be the hardest part of hearing God's call. Picking up the phone acknowledges, "I have a problem. I need help."

The choice is to hear God's voice today. His call is to acknowledge there is a problem, a demon. God promises he is with us to work for the good. What will you do with the power God has given you to choose?

Saturday • One of the great parts of the miracle of recovery is the peace that comes with letting go of the struggle. No longer do I have to pretend I have it all together. No longer do I need to be afraid someone will find out. No longer do I have to lie. Do I have a perfect recovery? No. Are there times the tiger is ready to bite? Yes. Are there times the old behaviors, the lying, and the anger seep into my day? Indeed!

What do I do then? I pray. I pray. I pray. I pray that God helps me remember the good in my life. I pray that God reminds me of the peace that comes in my relationship with him. I pray that God helps me remember that I can choose to succumb to the demon or live in that peace.

Will you recognize the good God works in your life? Will you celebrate that today? How?

Week 14: Conquerors

No, in all these things we are more than conquerors through him who loved us.–ROMANS 8:37

Sunday • We've bungled so many things by bad judgment, poor decisions, our shortcomings, and our downright failures. How can we possibly be conquerors? If anything, we see ourselves as "the biggest loser."

Yet here is Saint Paul telling us that we are *more* than conquerors. Not that we *should* be conquerors, not that we *will* be conquerors if only we try harder. We already *are* conquerors.

What in the world is he talking about? Is this some kind of positive, feel-good message? Absolutely not. This is how God identifies us. Why? Because in the life, death, and resurrection of Jesus Christ, he has won the victory and we—you and me, children of God, joint heirs—share in it. That is why we, who often mess up, can say, "I can do all things through Christ who strengthens me." Together, we can conquer!

Monday • Who do you think of as conquerors? Usually it is a term we associate with war and warriors. Maybe Attila the Hun or Genghis Khan or Alexander the Great—old guys with lots of troops and armament. The dictionary says it is someone who wins by a great deal of effort. And in this Scripture passage, Saint Paul says that we are *more* than conquerors. Conquerors of what? Conquerors of the parts of our lives that interfere with our relationship with God.

What parts of our lives interfere with our relationship with God? It's the parts that interfere with the commandment, "Love the Lord your God with all your heart and all your soul and all your mind…and your neighbor as yourself." What gets in the way of fulfilling this commandment? Perhaps it's things like greed (wanting more than we need, refusing to give to the poor), anger (yelling at our children, refusing to apologize to our spouse), lying (rationalizing and excusing our actions). All of these are things that interfere with our relationship with God—things we need to conquer.

Can you spend a few minutes today looking at something you struggle with—something that keeps you unsettled and agitated? Do you want to conquer it? Does it interfere with your relationship with God? How?

Tuesday • My sons are both career U.S. Marines. They are "warriors." I really don't think of them as conquerors, but they certainly have those traits. They are passionate about their role in world peace. They are skilled in their unique roles. They practice, practice, practice, train, train, train. They are prepared for all contingencies. Truthfulness and honesty are core values. They are deeply troubled when a fellow Marine does not maintain the honor of the Corps. They believe in the Marine Corps motto—*Semper Fidelis*—"Always faithful." They are passionate about the Marine Corps itself and their commitment to their fellow Marines. Those are the traits of conquerors.

Do we have those traits as people of faith, as conquerors? Do we have the traits to be always faithful to our God? Are we passionate about our faith? Do we practice and train—with prayer? Are we prepared for all contingencies if our enemies of greed, anger, lying, or addictions reenter our lives?

How? How today?

Wednesday • When we make up our mind to change, to conquer a behavior that is interfering with our relationship with God, we experience a sense of relief and release. But when we slip back into that old behavior, we're apt to feel defeated. We certainly don't feel like conquerors. When we find ourselves slipping back into the old thinking, the greed, the anger, the lying, the addiction, we feel defeated. The biggest loser.

But that is not the truth of our situation, and it's certainly not the truth of our faith. During the time we were working on our new behavior, we learned new ways of being. When we didn't buy that pair of shoes on sale but gave an extra offering in church that Sunday, it made a difference in how we felt. When we monitored our anger, we found we could change the words before they came out. When we told the truth, there were some consequences, but the world did not end. People began to trust us. When we stopped the drugs or alcohol, our bodies felt better, our minds cleared, and we found a support network.

None of this learning is wasted if we thank God for it...if we see it as a step toward conquering the demon. We take the learning and we move forward. The Spirit draws us on. We move forward in the promise that God works with us for our good. The love God has for us is our armament and our troops. We *are* more than conquerors.

Are you discouraged about winning a battle against something that interferes with your relationship with God? What have you learned so far that works? Where has God been in that learning?

Holy Thursday • We are able to make changes in our thinking and in our behavior because we are empowered by God. We do not do this stuff because we are so strong or such incredible people. We do not make changes in our lives by ourselves. We are able to make incredible changes in our lives *because* God gives us the grace and power. Too often we forget that part. We think we have done this all by ourselves. We become boastful about how much clean time we have. We think we have become this loving, generous person through our own efforts. We think we have all the answers to give to someone else. We use pat sayings and slogans as though they perform some kind of magic.

But it's God who works for the good in our lives. This must remain in our heart and soul. As Saint Paul says, "I can do all things through Christ who strengthens me."

Today, can you thank God for the changes he has empowered you to make? What changes? How has God empowered you?

Good Friday • As a child I was often encouraged to "give up" something during Lent—something I really liked and would miss. It was to remind me of the sacrifice Christ gave of his life so that I might be redeemed. I was to repent of my sins, and this was the penance. Those are words I recall as very important. And the words worked. I gave up candy and I gave up movies and I gave up arguing with my brother...well, sort of. And I thought of what Christ had done for me.

As an adult, another word that I find very powerful, especially during Lent, is *metanoia*. It's a Greek word that means opening our lives to the Spirit of God. When our lives are open to the Spirit of God, he empowers us to make the little changes that move us closer to who he wants us to be. As an adult, I still "give up" or "take on" something for Lent, but the part that moves with me after Lent and into the rest of my year and my life is when I focus, a prayerful focus, on opening my life to the little changes God holds out for me. It's not a change like Saint Paul had on the road to Damascus. I don't expect God to knock me off a horse and speak directly to me. But I pray that I will be open to his voice empowering me to make changes in my heart.

What small change might make a difference in your life? Maybe reconciling with a family member you have been cut off from for years? Forgiving a slight you hold as a resentment? Reaching out to a neighbor who is sick? Are you open to God's offer of change in your heart?

Holy Saturday • During World War II, Norway was conquered by Germany. The Norwegians were subjected to harsh, painful restrictions on movement, food, and the necessities of daily living. Their lives were grim and depressing. Their hope of freedom was banished for years. That is often the fate of those who are conquered. But finally the Allies were victorious in the landing at Normandy, and the tide of the war changed. The news of that victory reached the people of Norway. Nothing immediately changed in their daily lives, but once again they had hope—hope that they would be rescued, hope that they would again have freedom.

On this Holy Saturday, that is the hope we have. Nothing big may have changed in our lives these past six weeks, but we have the good news that there is hope. We have the good news that we are children of God. We are joint heirs to his kingdom. God works for our good. The Spirit intervenes for us...even groans with us. We are conquerors. We have freedom. We are rescued. The cross of ashes reminds us we are redeemed.

Can you begin to take this "Good News" into your heart? Can you begin to have the hope of freedom and redemption?

Easter: Jesus' Resurrection in Our Lives

Easter and the five weeks following consider the power of Christ's resurrection in our lives.

Week 15: Our Lord's Resurrection

For I am convinced that neither death, nor life, nor angels, nor rulers, nor things present, nor things to come, nor powers, nor height, nor depth, nor anything else in all creation, will be able to separate us from the love of God in Christ Jesus our Lord.

—ROMANS 8:38–39

Sunday • Romans 8 is one of the greatest chapters in all of Scripture. It contains a host of magnificent promises of God—promises that we both live by and die by. It begins with no condemnation and closes with no separation.

On this Easter Sunday, we want to reflect on what our Lord's resurrection has to say about separation and about us. When we stop to think about it, all kinds of things separate us from the love of Christ: sin, faithlessness, rebellion, indifference, and bitterness. From a human point of view, it would appear that these are the very things that could kill the love of Christ for us.

But not so, says Saint Paul. From a divine point of view, from God's point of view, nothing can separate us from Christ's love for us. He keeps coming for us. He is the risen Lord, so that means he is alive. He will never give up on us. He walks by our side and calls to us, inviting us back again to his love and forgiveness. He always welcomes us back, gently tells us our sins are forgiven, buried in his tomb. He lives to draw us close with the silk cords of his love.

Monday • In this part of Saint Paul's Letter to the Romans is the gift of God's promise of forgiveness and eternal love. By Christ's death and resurrection, he has redeemed us from our sins. Nothing can separate us from him. What a promise!

If we read articles about the resilience of children of divorce, we learn that children whose noncustodial parent is actively involved in their lives have much more chance of surviving the divorce with strength and success. Children whose noncustodial parent breaks the promise to spend time with them on the weekends or doesn't show up for promised outings often become depressed, angry, and rebellious. They feel rejected and unloved.

God is our parent. We call him "Abba, Father," and he never, ever breaks his promise to be there.

Do we forget God's promise that by his cross and resurrection he will always be with us and love us? Is that what happens when we are anxious and frightened?

Tuesday • I grew up believing that a lot of things I might do or even think could separate me from the love of Christ. Well-meaning parents and teachers created that misunderstanding by thinking they were teaching me right from wrong. "Christ won't love you if…" I unfortunately thought God would leave me because of my self-centeredness or my temper or my lies. What I didn't understand in those early years is that I was the one who turned away from God. God never turned away from me. That is his promise. His love is always there.

As an adult, it has been a beautiful awakening to have finally learned the promise of no separation/no condemnation. No matter what my sin is, no matter how I turn away from God, he does not leave me. My sin might offend him, might make him sad, but he is "always at my side." He does not condemn me to live apart from him. He does not separate from me.

During this Easter week, focus on the times Christ is at your side. Make note of them in a journal or on a calendar. Isn't it amazing?

Wednesday • A few years ago I was visiting my son and his family during Easter time. My six-year-old granddaughter, who was attending religious-education classes, asked me, "How did Christ come back from the dead? How could he appear to the Apostles? How could he walk through walls?"

Being somewhat taken aback by those questions but pleased that she was considering this incredible miracle, I wanted to give her some sense of the enormity of this mystery. So I said something about his appearance being in a different form from what we think of as standing right here in front of us. But I explained that no matter what that state was, his friends recognized him. And that's how he can be with us every day as well. "Sometimes," I said, "we don't completely understand God's being in our lives, but that's what he promises us."

That response seemed to satisfy her, and it also gave me an opportunity to consider what this promise of the resurrection means in my life...every day.

What does Christ's resurrection mean in your life...every day?

Thursday • Saint Paul says that neither angels nor rulers, nor heights, nor depths can keep us from Christ's love. In other words, *nothing*!

We talk frequently about demons in these meditations. That's what I think Saint Paul means by rulers. Though a demon sometimes refers to an addiction, it also means all the weaknesses and anxieties that rule us—that separate us from God's love. When we lose our way and slip back into old patterns, such as greed, lying, judgment, and gossip, it may feel as though God has left us and we're alone. We're separated from God. But as the Sunday devotion says, "God keeps coming for us."

Again, my favorite Psalm 139 reinforces God's covenant with us: "If I ascend to heaven, you are there; if I make my bed in Sheol, you are there." Relapse into our old behaviors feels like the depths of hell...feels like everyone has given up on us...feels like we have given up on ourselves. Not so. In the resurrection, Christ comes for us.

What demons do you feel keep you "separated" from God? How does Christ's resurrection close that gap for you?

Friday • One week ago on Good Friday, we focused on Christ crucified. We considered the pain and suffering of Christ and even the time he felt forsaken when he cried out to his Father. Many of us know how "forsaken" feels. We know what it feels like to be alone and afraid. Today, one week later, we focus on the risen Christ—Christ alive and among us—today, not just 2,000 years ago.

When we relapse, when we get stuck in our old behaviors, it's easy to feel forsaken. We feel that heavy despair of Good Friday. But today we live on the other side of the cross. We have seen the resurrected Christ. We are redeemed, forgiven, loved. We were broken. Now we are blessed.

Do you know Christ's blessing? Is it in your life? How? When?

Saturday • Many of us have images of the stone rolled back from Christ's grave on Easter morning. Those images might have come from holy cards we received or an illustrated children's book. We knew the burial cloths were rolled up inside and an angel said, "He is not here. He is risen." But few of us considered that our sins were sealed in that tomb when it was closed again. To think of our sins permanently sealed beyond anyone's reach creates such a freeing thought. Christ will "remember them no more."

Others in our lives may remember our sins and may even remind us of them from time to time. But when we can picture those sins as permanently removed from God's sight and mind, we know we are free...free to live God's forgiveness and grace with others. Our sins are forgiven. They are sealed and will never be reviewed or evaluated or judged by God. He has come after us and draws us close.

Can you picture that tomb? Are you open to those images of your own failures and shortcomings sealed up forever?

Week 16: Immeasurable Power

...and what is the immeasurable greatness of his power for us who believe, according to the working of his great power. God put this power to work in Christ when he raised him from the dead. —EPHESIANS 1:19–20

Sunday • The Church has a rather strange way of figuring out when Easter comes. Christian Tradition says we celebrate Easter on the first Sunday after the full moon that happens upon or next after March 21; and if the full moon happens on a Sunday, Easter is the Sunday after. How convoluted. But perhaps there's another way to figure this out.

Easter comes when we open our lives to God's resurrection power. Saint Paul tells us in Ephesians that the same divine, creative energy that raised Christ from the dead is available to us right now. Listen carefully: The power that shattered death for Jesus, the power that caused Christ to be alive this very moment, that power is ours to help us live.

We don't need to live defeated lives any longer; the risen Christ is here to give us the victory. Nor do we need to continue to live boring lives; Christ is here to lead us on the path of discipleship. No longer need we live under the tyranny of sin; Christ has broken the grip of sin on our lives. No longer need we live under the cloud of death; Christ has smashed the power of death and has given us the gift of everlasting life.

When does Easter come? It comes when we open our hearts to the power of the risen Christ.

Monday • In Sunday's devotion, we talked about the divine, creative energy that raised Christ from the dead as being available to us as well. I grew up believing I was not very creative. I got good grades in school, but much of that was just reciting facts. I fouled up many attempts at cooking. (I once found my brother giving the dog some eggs I had cooked for him.) My mother made me rip out every seam I ever sewed (or so it seemed). I still envy people who cook gourmet meals, knit beautiful scarves, paint in oils, and dress with fashion and style—all seemingly without effort.

But later in my life after I had completed an oral presentation in graduate school, a teacher and mentor said, "Penny, you are so creative." I heard those words over twenty years ago, and I remember the occasion like it was yesterday. Words are powerful!

I have come to believe we are given "divine, creative energy" because of Christ's resurrection. We are given that energy to live new lives and to make the shifts in our thoughts and behaviors that lead us into powerful relationship with Christ. These words change our lives.

Do you have a sense of God's creative power in your life? Where? Does it have a sense of the divine? Do you sense the energy it gives?

Tuesday • In today's world we hear much about natural energy and created energy and the power grid and where we will get the power to heat our homes, light our factories, and fill our cars. The same holds for our lives. Where will we get the energy to sustain the lives Christ opens for us?

In my book about recovery from addiction, I talk about three stages of healing. I believe these stages and the healing they represent are applicable to many of our demons and to areas in our lives that we wish to change. Change and healing take energy—divine, creative energy. In the first stage of change, we name the problem. It's tough to name the problem because when we do, we might have to do something about it. In the second stage, we work on modifying behaviors and shifting our thinking. It's difficult and tiring to modify behaviors and pay close attention to our thinking and behavior. In stage three, we work on our relationship with God, which sustains us in our recovery. And it's scary to open ourselves up to a new relationship with God. It might mean we have to give up some old habits.

The miracle of change and healing and living this new life is that it happens through God's divine, creative energy. Through this new energy, we become empowered to make changes…to give us the heat and the light of a new life. Today every time you switch on a light or start your car or get on a bus or turn on your stove or work on your computer or charge a cell phone, think of the energy it takes for you to live your life.

What divine energy do you need to move closer to the life Christ wants for you?

Wednesday • When that teacher told me many years ago that I was creative, it shifted my thinking. It completely altered the image I had of myself. Though it didn't erase all the old messages, it gave me the freedom to consider myself differently. Maybe I didn't have to continue to see myself as a cookie-cutter student, wife, mother, and nurse. Maybe I could "think outside the box." Maybe along with this new healing, I could step out into a new way of living. Maybe I could say "no" to some expectations. After all, "no" is a complete sentence! Maybe I could say "yes" to some new adventures.

We often stay stuck in our old lives because of early messages we have received about who we are. But when we become more open to the messages of God's divine, creative love, we get glimpses of new ways of living. My shifts were empowered, not just by one message, but by subtle whispers that I could change and that God was in my life to walk with me in those changes.

In this Easter season, do you hear whispers of divine, creative energy, of his immeasurable power? Are you listening for them?

Thursday • Sunday's devotion encourages us to consider that Christ's resurrection leads us to a life of discipleship. Now, *disciple* is not a word I would have used to describe myself in years past. From my early education, I considered disciples as people who were with Christ during his life. They were people who took the teachings of Christ to those who had not heard of him.

But the more contemporary way to think of discipleship is in a path of service. Now again, I used to think of service as working in my church, being a lector, or serving in the soup kitchen in our community. Another way to consider service is a service connected with love. It can be a service of forgiving others, a service of letting go of resentments, a service of speaking in a loving manner, a service of no gossip.

Discipleship is empowered by Christ's divine, creative energy.

Do you consider yourself a disciple of Christ? What does that mean for your self-identity? Are you empowered?

Friday • When we are stuck in our old lives, lives made up of anxieties, vulnerabilities, and fears, it can feel as if we were dead. At minimum, it feels like we are in a coma. We can hear what is going on outside, but we have no energy to respond, no energy to let anyone know we hear, no energy to do anything differently. We might be breathing and responding to "deep stimuli," but it certainly does not feel like living. We are spiritually dead. Christ's resurrection is the healing energy to pull us back into life. He is here now, today. His resurrection gives us the power to respond to what is around us.

What would it take to move you out of the coma?

Saturday • No matter what the date of Easter, it always comes in the spring. It comes just as most of us yearn for warmer weather. We wait for the daffodils and tulips, for the trees to bud. Easter arrives with bunnies and chicks and new life.

One year when my children were very young and still believed the Easter bunny brought their baskets of eggs and candy, I put talcum powder on the rug in the shape of bunny paw prints. My not-yet three-year-old son was in awe. I have a picture of his puzzlement that still makes me smile. He believed in that bunny for years!

Easter can be puzzling. I see Christ's tracks after resurrection, and I am in awe. And what a gift that Easter comes in springtime when God gives us all these signs of new life. How much clearer can those prints be?

Do you believe?

Week 17: The Word Is "Life"

Jesus said to her, "I am the resurrection and the life. Those who believe in me, even though they die, will live, and everyone who lives and believes in me will never die. Do you believe this?"

—JOHN 11:25–26

Sunday • Suppose you had the opportunity to choose a place—any place—to hold an Easter service. What location would you pick? One place I'd choose would be a cemetery. Is there a graveyard somewhere that holds someone you really loved—a father or mother perhaps, a sweetheart, a child, a brother or sister? Can you remember the pain you felt when the body was slowly lowered into the ground? Can you still recall the terrible ache you felt? Perhaps you feel it even as you read these words. You can still remember the horrible sense of loss and loneliness and emptiness. Graves seem so final, don't they?

That's why I would hold an Easter service at the cemetery. Easter means that death does not have the final word. Our Lord's open grave on Easter morning means he has the last word, and that word is *life*. The risen Christ has conquered death. He has taken the pain out of the grave; he has destroyed its power. He has broken its grip on us.

Listen to what he says: "I am the resurrection and the life. Those who believe in me, even though they die, will live, and everyone who lives and believes in me will never die."

How's *that* for Good News?

Monday • Have you celebrated any memorable Easter services? I remember one Easter sunrise service on a military base in South Carolina where the sand fleas rose with the sun and I couldn't concentrate on the service because of the terrible itching on my ankles. There have been services on mountaintops trying to capture the miracle of sunrise and resurrection. There have been Easter Vigils with darkened churches and bonfires and candles. There have been services in private living rooms with a small gathering, maybe like the first Apostles, not even aware of the miracle of the resurrection.

All of these services have marked the resurrection of Christ... the Good News. To have an Easter Mass or service in the grave-yard of my daughter or parents would be a powerful connection to God's promise that there is life after this life—probably one we cannot even fathom. But God has promised everlasting life through Christ's resurrection. Christ asks Lazarus' sister, "Do you believe?"

Perhaps you'd like to pray, "Lord, I believe; help my unbelief!" (Mark 9:24).

Tuesday • One of the most incredible Easter mornings I ever experienced was not a service at all. I was vacationing with family on a North Carolina beach. Everyone else was still asleep, but I walked down to the ocean to watch the sun come up. As I approached the beach I noted that the moon was setting to the west, and when I stood facing east, here came the sun. The moon setting to my back, the sun rising to the east. I stood there surrounded by this shining metaphor I will never forget. My sins, my past setting, were behind me, and my new life was rising before me.

Since that morning I have heard that this setting moon and rising sun—or setting sun and rising moon—are natural, though infrequent, astronomical events. People gather and schedule to be where this is visible. For me, it was a once-in-a-lifetime Easter Sunday image of resurrection and new life.

Do you have a personal image of resurrection? What does it mean to you?

Wednesday • There have been other Easter times and other Easter seasons that have made a difference in my prayer life, in my faith, in my relationship with God. While living in Chicago for two years, I attended Old St. Pat's, a vibrant, dynamic parish located in the Loop. The homily message each Sunday underscored that I was forgiven, that I was a beloved daughter of God. I must have heard that message before, but there I received it in a new way.

This dynamic parish had active Lenten discussions and services. On Holy Thursday they had communal dinners and

Eucharist to commemorate the Last Supper. Following supper, we walked into the darkened church for reconciliation—group and private. This service, both dinner and reconciliation, was so popular that attendees had to make reservations weeks before.

For me, all of this preparation was part of the Easter experience. It helped me to better focus on the entire Lenten and Easter season. I felt included. I was part of the Passion, and that helped me partake in the miracle of the resurrection. The popularity of this parish and of this Lenten and Easter experience made me realize how many of us long for this kind of active, inclusive life with Christ.

Do you also long for a more active spiritual life?

Thursday • The experience of the church in Chicago helped center me in my faith. Though I had attended Mass regularly all my life, my adult faith education was sadly lacking. I was a sixth-grade Catholic-school graduate, and my knowledge of my beliefs and even of my Church had ended at about age twelve. In the intervening years, my parents had both died and my twelve-year-old daughter was killed in a traffic accident. The pain of death seeped into many days. I clung to the old teachings but longed for a deeper understanding of life, of death, of God's promises. The old faith based on "Sister said it was so" simply wasn't working anymore. I longed for a more active spiritual life.

And by one of those quiet miracles, God put me in Chicago where that more active spiritual life began. I don't live in Chicago any longer, and I miss Old St. Pat's terribly. But what I learned there, besides Scripture and prayer and community and relationship with God, is that I can find that active spiritual life in other places. I find it at a Benedictine priory nearby where antiphonal prayer is sung many times a day. I find it in the monks' singing and recordings I can play to soothe myself. I find it in challenging myself with new books, some about life and death. I find it in daily morning devotion and meditation. I find it in the local parish workshops and seminars.

Can you do one thing this week to make your spiritual life more active? Is there one area of your faith that troubles you, that you have questions about? Can you search for some understanding of that issue? When?

Friday • When we think of death, we think of the grief process. Mental-health professionals tell us that grieving involves denial, anger, bargaining, depression, and acceptance. Though teaching about that process is changing, the bottom line is that before a person can heal, at some point the grieving person has to "accept" the loss of the loved one. Don't tell a newly grieving person that! To a person experiencing the recent loss of a loved one, the pain of grieving is better than the idea of acceptance. Acceptance conjures up the idea that the loved one is gone forever.

Christ's resurrection tells us that when we believe in his promise, we will not die. That means our loved one is not gone forever. Somehow in ways we cannot understand, God has destroyed death's power. We come to grips with the reality that the person is no longer in our daily lives. We make adjustments. We remember with less pain. We begin to laugh again. We don't forget. We are not afraid.

What loved one has died and made a difference in your daily life? Are you less afraid?

Saturday • Death does not have the final word. The cemetery does not have the final word. Christ's resurrection has the final word. Christ is the word, the way, the truth, and the light. I live in his promise, "Do not fear, for I have redeemed you; I have called you by name, you are mine" (Isaiah 43:1). Please pray this at my funeral!

What images come to mind when you think about death?

Week 18: A New Creation

Whoever is in Christ is a new creation: the old things have passed away; behold, new things have come. –2 CORINTHIANS 5:17 *(NAB)*

Sunday • The resurrection of Christ explodes a bunch of myths we hang on to. One such myth is the notion that people don't or can't change. It's the "you can't teach an old dog new tricks" mentality.

Now that is an easy myth to buy in to. We examine our lives, and we wonder how much closer we are to what God wants us to be since we first began our journey of faith. It's disappointing, isn't it? It's easy to believe that we are what we are. We say, "I'll never change no matter how hard I try." We believe that our patterns of behavior, thinking, and responding to others are so deeply engraved that we are destined to live with them.

That is a myth and a terrible piece of fiction. Christ is risen, and the very same power that brought his lifeless body from the grave is the same power available to us here and now. It makes no difference how often we have failed or how miserable our past has been. It makes no difference how far we have fallen or how frequently we have messed up. It doesn't even matter how set we are in our ways. No matter what, the risen Christ will not be defeated. He is eager to work his miracles in our lives, and he will do it. He promises to do it.

Monday • In my book on addiction, I identify six issues that I believe make recovery a challenge. In exploring those issues and making changes, a person in recovery decreases the power those issues have as stumbling blocks to long-term recovery. Though the book explores those issues from a woman's perspective, the implications for change are applicable to both men and women. God works with us to modify our behaviors and our entrenched thinking. This week we will touch briefly on those six issues: self-image, traditional roles, ineffective communication, grief and loss, medical aspects, abuse and anger.

Self-image: As children, our self-image comes from the messages we receive about ourselves from adults. For better or worse, we come to believe that is who and what we are. As adults, that image shifts depending on our successes and failures. We judge ourselves as a success or as a failure, or somewhere on that continuum. We stand tall, or we slump.

If our image is one of not living up to what God wants us to be, how do we begin to change that image and live a new life? How do we use the power of the risen Christ? One way is to change the old messages we heard as a child—the ones that called us stupid or a nerd or skinny or fat. We hear those messages and we change them. We focus on a new message, a new image that says, "I am a beloved child of God."

The world says, "Yes!" to you. Do you hear the new message? *The old is gone, the new has come.*

Tuesday • *Traditional roles:* When we look at the roles we play in our lives, we sometimes sit back and say, "How did I get here?" Or, "I didn't ask for this." That's true. Often our lives and our duties and our roles just seem to happen. We follow traditional expectations and make choices that seem minor at the time, yet they change the trajectory of our lives and limit our choices down the road.

Sometimes the frustration, irritation, and even anger at the roles we find ourselves in lead us to make excuses for returning to our old behaviors. We are all in recovery from something, some addiction or habit that pulls us away from God. None of us is perfect, and we can no longer rationalize, "That is just the way I am." In this new life, we use the creative energy and power given to us from the resurrected Christ to begin to see our roles as sacred. Christ is with us to give us the courage to see the wonder in our days. With his help, we begin to see the wonder in God's blessing of us. We use that blessing to treasure the moments with our family, to thank God for the food we can cook, to thank God for the car in which we chauffeur the kids, to thank God for clothes we can wash, to thank God for the home we can clean, to thank God for the job we have. We begin to understand the sacredness of our roles.

What task do you have today that irritates you the most? What part of it is a gift? What part of it is sacred? *The old is gone, the new has come.*

Wednesday • *Ineffective communication:* When we can't communicate effectively, we create tension, stress, and anxiety in our lives. Our difficulty in asking for what we need, our difficulty in expressing our feelings, our difficulty in listening—really listening—to others are at the root of so many triggers for relapse. Ineffective communication keeps us out of relationship with others and with God. We wind up feeling alone and lonely. We ask, "Why bother?"

How do we change our communication? How do we find the courage to ask for what we need, to express our feelings, and ultimately to "shut up and listen"? We learn new strategies, we ask for help, we quiet our minds and pray to hear God's whisper.

Recall your conversations today. What do you wish you had said differently? Can you go back and modify that? *The old is gone, the new has come.*

Thursday • *Grief and loss:* Loss infuses our lives with sadness and guilt. The loss of a loved one, the loss of a job, the loss of a belief in who we are can be issues that set us up for a retreat into all the old destructive coping mechanisms. The emptiness that accompanies the death of a spouse or parent or child leaves a gaping hole, a palpable pain. The guilt associated with any grief and loss is a recording in our heads not easily erased. Over and over we hear, "If only...if only...if only."

The message needs to be recorded differently. General guilt is OK; it keeps us on the straight and narrow. It is our conscience talking to us—the Holy Spirit in our lives. But the destructive tapes of "if only..." set us up for depression and a mistrust of God's message of forgiveness. We can't forgive ourselves. Frederick Buechner says trying to forgive ourselves is like trying to sit in our own lap.

What destructive, meaningless message of guilt do you continue to beat yourself up with? What new message of God's divine, creative energy and power do you need to replace it with? You are God's beloved child. All is forgiven. His promise. *The old is gone, the new has come.*

Friday • *Medical aspects:* Our bodies are a good place to begin change. When we are caught in the cycle of addiction and other destructive patterns, we tend to ignore taking care of our bodies. We eat more of the bad stuff. We don't have the energy to exercise. We put off an annual physical exam or mammogram or even the dentist. Once we hear the whisper that we have the power to make change in our lives, we have a responsibility to do that. We are response-able (able to respond) to God's whisper that our lives can be different. We have been given the incredible gift of our bodies. We are to take that responsibility seriously.

Again we make little choices. We cut down on the sugar and the fried foods and the cans of soda. We walk the six blocks to the supermarket. We make the appointment for the physical exam. And as those small choices begin to clear our heads, we make further commitments to diet, exercise, and weight loss. We cut out the cigarettes. What money we save! Even local hospitals give free smoke-ending clinics and provide the patches for free. It is possible.

You are empowered by Christ's resurrection.

What small change will you begin today? Write it on a calendar. Write it for the whole week…for the whole month. Each morning ask God to remind you of the power he has given you—the power to follow through with that change. *The old is gone, the new has come.*

Saturday • *Abuse and anger:* As many as 75 percent of women who are addicted to drugs have been abused. The anger they feel as a consequence of that abuse lurks beneath the surface and then often erupts in ways that are as destructive, painful, and harmful as the abuse itself. The anger defines who they are and how they respond and relate to other people. It might not look like anger. It might look more like depression. It might look like promiscuity. It might look like shoplifting. It might look like getting high daily. However it looks, it never looks good.

Working through the anger is a long, slow process. But it's the only way to come out the other side with a sense of relief and peace. How do we do that? We begin a process of learning to forgive. Rev. Desmond Tutu, a black man imprisoned and beaten in white South Africa for years, has written a model of forgiveness. Some highlights from that model are worth repeating:

1. We need to forgive, but we do not need to forget. In fact, we need to remember so we do not repeat the abuse.
2. We move to forgiveness, but we hold that person accountable.
3. We make an effort to walk in the shoes of the abuser and try to understand the pressures that have shaped them.
4. We give up the desire for revenge. Revenge can poison our soul. (*No Future With Forgiveness*, Tutu, D., 1999)

Tutu says that when we are able to move into forgiveness, we are able to write the end of the story. We are able to forgive because we have been forgiven. What will you do today with the gift and power of forgiveness? You are not alone. *The old is gone, the new has come.*

Week 19: Gracious Presence

No one has ever seen God. It is God the only Son, who is close to the Father's heart, who has made him known.–JOHN 1:18

Sunday • Another myth the resurrection explodes is the notion that God is too distant or remote for us to know on a personal and intimate basis. The modern version of that claim is, "God is not dead. He just doesn't want to get involved."

Have you ever felt that way? Have you ever felt that God is too transcendent and too far removed to be available to you? That you are an insignificant speck and that he has much bigger and more important things to deal with? Have you ever felt that you are essentially left on your own to make it the best you can?

That's a myth. To live in a world where Christ is risen is to live in a world where he is our contemporary. That means you are daily sustained by the gracious presence of the risen Lord. He is there to share with you in the task of turning the world upside down for his sake. Christ is alive. He is risen, and he is with you now. Not even the gates of hell can prevail against you.

Monday • As a child in parochial school, I learned about a God who, for me, was both a majesty far removed and a crucifix in the classroom. It was a bit of a mystery. How could God be up there in heaven and down here in the classroom?

His presence still sometimes remains a mystery to me. I pray to sense his presence and I see it in the beauty of the world he has created: the fresh snow on the ground, the first daffodils after a long winter, and the precious first smiles of a grandchild. I see God's majesty all around me. And I pray to sense his presence in the frantic drive to work, in the irritable coworker, in the tired grocery-store clerk.

And often I beg for his presence when I'm afraid. I ask God to be close when a friend is awaiting a lab report, when a child is hurt, when the addiction rears its ugly head. Does God really care? Is he really involved in my life? If he cares enough to create the beauty around me, wouldn't he care enough to be with me, his beloved child? If I would drop everything to be with one of my children in trouble, wouldn't God do the same and so much more?

Where is God showing you his presence in your life—today?

Tuesday • Unfortunately as children, we heard teachings about God and Christ that often had an element of fear attached to them. We heard of punishment and hell and damnation, and somehow that was louder than love and forgiveness and grace. Then there were the stories of God's power and might. We heard of God's anger and wrath—all pretty frightening for a child—and fear of God was the outcome. So many Scripture readings talk about "fear of the Lord." The thought of a loving God personally involved in my life on a daily basis was something I had to grow in to. Shifting that word of *fear* to *awe* has also been a process of study, reflection, and prayer.

I pray to daily feel God's presence, to not fear his punishment. I ask to know God's forgiveness and to feel the peace that surpasses all understanding. I listen when God whispers, and I laugh when he shows up in unexpected ways.

How can you move from fear to awe, from fear of a wrathful God to awe of his majesty to delight in his ways?

Wednesday • It's easy for us to slip in to paying attention to God only on Sundays. Work, family, and conversation consume the rest of the week with friends, exercise. It's way too easy in this world of 24-7 television, iPods, iPhones, BlackBerries, and some new toy every few months to keep us otherwise occupied—occupied with something other than our relationship with God. What if we had another relationship we were trying to build? Would it work to drop by once a week for an hour, think about other stuff while the other person was attempting to carry on a meaningful conversation with us, smile, and leave? Then we'd return the next week but with no calls or attention to that person during the week. Try that with a new girlfriend or boyfriend!

It's not God who isn't paying attention. It's not God who is uninvolved in our lives. It's us who don't take the time to notice that he's right here—every single minute of every day.

You are taking time today to feel God's presence simply by the few minutes you spend reading this. How else might you take time today to feel God's presence?

Thursday • One of the times it feels most like God is not present in our lives, and maybe in our world, is when tragedy happens: an earthquake, a tsunami, the death of a loved one. There is such an emptiness, an abyss. A friend wonders how she can ever forgive herself for some decisions she made during the dying of a loved one. I spoke with her about gaining a sense of God's forgiveness. I reminded her that his forgiveness gives us the freedom to accept ourselves, our decisions, and moves us to peace. She said, "But what if I don't really have that kind of faith, that belief in God?" And at that moment I had a new understanding of what it means to not have any real sense of God in one's daily life. I had no answer to give her if she doesn't have a belief in God's presence somewhere in her life. I could give her the usual psychobabble I learned as a therapist, but I found that was really only a small bandage.

Granted, on some days I struggle like everyone else with doubts about God's presence; but when I feel most alone, when I see myself at the edge of the abyss, I know God is with me. I know that if I quiet myself and bring some part of myself into his presence, he will take my hand.

What do you say to someone who is struggling and in pain and has no sense that God is there?

Friday • The Sunday devotion encourages us to consider the risen Christ as our contemporary. Now my relationship with some of my contemporaries is wonderful, and some of those relationships take a lot of work. This relationship with Christ can also take some work. It has its ups and downs, its days of closeness and days of distance. There are days when I find the notion that God wants to work with me in turning this world upside down absolutely ludicrous.

But when I consider that notion from a different perspective, that is absolutely what a life of discipleship means: turning the world upside down with God's power. This power could be as easy as the power to smile at the bus driver, the power to speak gently to my husband when he is about to drive me nuts, the power to give an hour to a caregiver friend who needs to get a haircut, the power to reach out again and again to people affected by a disaster. That is how we are to turn the world upside down: through the power of Christ's resurrection.

How will you turn the world upside down today? How will you know it is Christ's power that is helping you do this?

Saturday • When I started to write this book, I wrestled with the fear that I would not find 365 different things to say about life, Scripture, God's presence, struggles, challenges, anxieties, addictions—how it all fits together, or doesn't. Where would the ideas come from? Would I find the right words? I struggled for a few weeks, and nothing seemed to come together. Then my husband and I talked about the format these devotions now take: a Scripture passage, a Sunday devotion reflecting on that passage's spiritual meaning, and then daily reflections throughout the week on how this might apply to our lives.

When I began writing, I was surprised that the ideas just seemed to flow. It was like a faucet had opened and there was a gentle stream of thoughts. I laughingly said, "I think the Holy Spirit is in this house. Don't open the door lest he or she escape." And though I was somewhat joking, I think that is exactly what happened here and what happens with you. I smile and believe the Holy Spirit is "write" here.

Where is the Holy Spirit in your life today? Does that surprise you? Can you be surprised by the joy that brings?

Week 20: Christ's Victory

"Where, O death, is your victory? Where, O death, is your sting?"
The sting of death is sin, and the power of sin is the law.

–1 CORINTHIANS 15:55–56

Sunday • The last myth the resurrection of Christ lays bare is the idea that death rules us, that death always has the last word, that death is "king." Perhaps you've been at the graveside of a loved one and were fighting to hold back the tears, convinced that death had won and that there was absolutely nothing beyond the coffin and grave.

But that is a lie. Christ is risen. The tomb could not hold him. The stone has been rolled away. The grim power of death has been destroyed. The poisonous sting has been removed. There is, in fact, life beyond the grave, and death is just a gateway that leads us into a new life filled with joy and in which there is no pain or sorrow—a new life in which we are in the presence of the risen Christ. The resurrection of Christ means that not death but God has the final word. And this is a word that enables us to face death with grace and courage and without fear. It is a word that enables us to walk through the valley of the shadow of death and fear no evil. It is a word that enables us to say, "Surely goodness and mercy shall follow me all the days of my life, and I shall dwell in the house of the LORD my whole life long" (Psalm 23:6). The risen Christ has the final message: "Because I live, you also will live" (John 14:19).

Monday • The first death of a loved one that I experienced was the death of our daughter in a car accident. This was an event that was total, final, and absolute. There was no sense in praying for a different outcome. She was dead. That would not change. I had been a nurse for fifteen years, but nothing prepared me for the enormity of the pain I experienced. It felt impossible to pray, "Thy will be done." How could this be God's will? She was gone—gone where?

I believed in God. I believed in heaven. I believed in a life hereafter. With all my heart I knew this precious child was with God. But how was I going to live my life without her?

I longed to grow. I needed answers. And after years and years, I find there are answers. I learned that God is with me in everything I experience. Through Christ's resurrection, he promises me that the evil, the pain, the sadness, the emptiness, the anger, will not overtake me. They won't rule my life. God will walk with me if only I will turn and take his hand. After years, the pain begins to lessen. The waves of guilt, remorse for things not done, words not spoken, begin to subside and get further and further apart. Those waves are replaced with a sense of God's presence in my life.

Is there a loss or death in your life that feels like the end? Today, can you pray for a sense of God's presence to fill that void?

Tuesday • When one moves into a "certain age," the natural death of family and friends becomes a more common occurrence. But each death, no matter the person's age, is a loss. Nothing about it seems "natural." My mother was eighty-eight years old when she died. Her life had been one of good physical health but infused with sadness, guilt, and anxiety. That sadness and guilt and the turmoil caused by my father's alcoholism played itself out in her need to control her surroundings. Cleanliness was nearly an obsession and interfered with relationships and any sense of fun. In the final years of her life, things calmed down and she greatly enjoyed her friends and a good game of bridge. Counting trump and controlling the game was right up her alley!

One thing my mother prayed for was a "peaceful death." It was part of her early prayer life, part of the novenas she prayed. And her prayers were answered. On her deathbed, truly hours before she died, she looked at me and said, "I'm not afraid." Oh, that we should all have that faith!

At your death will you be able to say, "I'm not afraid"? What would it take to move toward that peace?

Wednesday • The anxiety that fills many of us about our death has to do with regrets of things not done plus fear of the dying itself. We move into our more senior years wondering where it all went. What happened to the dreams? And as we contemplate our death, we worry that we will be a burden to those we love and that our death will be painful.

From a psychological perspective, we can diminish some of the regrets. We still have time. What things would you like to do with the time you have left? You may not be able to have it all. You may not reach all of those young idealistic goals, but what parts of it can you still do?

The anxiety, the fear of being a burden, of terrible pain as we die, crosses our thoughts as we move into adulthood. That anxiety becomes more consuming as we age. The "shadow of death" lurks. Do we remember that Christ promises that by his resurrection, he has won victory over our death? He has taken the sting, the pain, out of our death. He promises to be with us, to help us face the process of dying with grace and courage.

Do you believe Christ will be with you at the time of your death? When you consider that in your heart, what happens?

Thursday • I recall a time when a family member died. During his dying process, he was an angry and abusive man. This was not new behavior, but it followed him into his process of dying with a vengeance. He berated the nurses, social workers, and family members about his care and his adamant demand to be taken home. Home was not an option for many care reasons. Finally he was moved to hospice and died calmly within a few days.

The saying "We die as we live" was incredibly evident during this man's dying process. We have choices, even in our dying. We can remain frightened and angry, or we can reach out our hand to God and ask that he give us grace and courage by knowing he is with us.

My friend's grandmother died with these words on her lips, "Jesus, I see you. I'm coming."

How do you envision your death? How do you envision your life? You have choices.

Friday • The Scripture reading this week says, "The sting of death is sin." If one definition of sin is the behavior and thoughts that distance us from God, those things that get in the way of our relationship with God, then we experience death each time we sin. Each time we feel anxiety when we know we are not doing the loving thing, when we know we are offending God, those are times we die a little. Each sin might not feel like a death, but sin can become a pattern—a series of choices that leads us further and further away from the life God wishes for us. And when I am distant from God, I try to fill that emptiness with all the wrong things. I am restless. I am not at peace.

Each day I can grow toward a life that is full and peaceful and blessed. Each day I can grow toward a death that is full and peaceful and blessed.

Take a few moments today to consider how your thoughts and behavior move you away from sin and toward a stronger relationship with God.

Saturday • At some level, we all know we are going to die. We don't know what comes after, but we have hope. Hope is of things not seen but promised. We have God's promise that he is with us. We have Christ's resurrection. We trust God will give us the strength and courage at the time. Just as he gave the Israelites manna in the desert when they needed it, he will give us strength when the time comes. But God gave it to them day by day—not for the month ahead—just as they needed it. So he doesn't give us strength today for what we need at our death, but he promises he will give it to us then.

What do you sense when you think of dwelling in the house of the Lord? Is there a sense of peace?

Post-Pentecost: The Holy Spirit Within Us

The nine weeks following Pentecost focus on the Holy Spirit within us.

Week 21: God's Power

When the day of Pentecost had come, they were all together in one place. And suddenly from heaven there came a sound like the rush of a violent wind, and it filled the entire house where they were sitting. Divided tongues, as of fire, appeared among them, and a tongue rested on each of them. All of them were filled with the Holy Spirit and began to speak in other languages, as the Spirit gave them ability.–ACTS 2:3–4

Sunday • Pentecost is one of the great festivals of the Church. Not only does it mark the Church's birthday but it also reminds us of the fulfillment of Christ's promise to pour out the Spirit upon his people...you...us. That truth gives rise to the very practical question, What do we have when we have the Spirit of Christ living within us?

The thing we have is the wind of God's power at our backs. His power is essential to our walking in the way of discipleship. Many of us who bear the name of Christ, Christian, often experience great frustration and discouragement. We want to do the Father's will, but we seem to lack the power to translate that desire into specific, concrete action. We make a resolution to do better, but we fail. Often we live defeated lives. We feel the God-shaped void.

Christ very clearly says that it is absolutely unnecessary for us to live defeated lives. The power to change is within reach.

The power is divine and supernatural; it is resurrection and miraculous power. With the Spirit, there is no reason you can't become the person Christ redeemed you to be. You can experience the fruits of the Spirit's power: self-control, joy, and a host of others. With the Spirit you can say with Paul, "I can do all things through [Christ] who strengthens me" (Philippians 4:13).

Monday • What do you think of when you picture a great festival? I think of Mardi Gras and parades and floats and beads and cakes and laughter. If Pentecost is the birthday of the Church, don't you wonder why we don't make a festival of it? Children love their birthdays. It is their personal festival. They count the days to it, and their eyes become bright with excitement. For years, psychologists have told us to get in touch with our "inner child," to hold on to delight.

At the birthday of the Church, Pentecost, we are the ones who have received the incredible gift of the Holy Spirit. It is the birthday of the Church, but we get the gift. Have we even unwrapped it? Or do we think of Pentecost as some strange occurrence involving wind and fire 2,000 years ago that happened only to the Apostles?

As you consider the festival of Pentecost, are you aware of the gift you have received? What gift? When?

Tuesday • Sunday's devotion encourages us to consider what we have when the Spirit of Christ is "living within us." Often the picture I have of Pentecost is of tongues of fire over the heads of the Apostles. But Scripture goes on to describe the miraculous power given the Apostles to speak in various languages that everyone could understand. The power represented by the tongues of fire did not just hover over the heads of the Apostles and then disappear. The power of the Spirit came to live within the Apostles.

My husband was taken to the hospital emergency room after he fainted during a bout with the flu. At the ER, he was given intravenous bags of fluid "to fill up his tank," as the doctor put it. Once he received those IVs, he could stand and walk and joke. The fluid immediately replenished his body with everything it needed.

That is what the Spirit of Christ living in us does. It enters our lives. It gives us strength from within. It's not just some power out there waiting to be called on. It is there, within us, all the time. Unfortunately, a good part of the time we don't even realize it's there. We ignore it until our "tank is too low."

Are you aware of the Spirit of Christ living in you? Isn't that just incredible? Pay attention to that today. Where do you become aware of it? Do you name it?

Wednesday • If we fail to notice the Holy Spirit within us, it's like receiving a gift on our birthday and never opening it. Who ever heard of such a thing? Certainly no child would ever pass up opening a gift. They dig right in. If it's something to eat, they eat it. If it's a toy, they begin playing with it. But sometimes as adults, we open a gift and then put it away. It's so beautiful or so extravagant that we want to save it. We don't even know what we are saving it for, but we don't want to spoil it.

The power of the Holy Spirit is not to be put away on a shelf. What do you think it's like to be the person giving the gift and realize the recipient never uses it, never enjoys it? When we give a gift, we want to see the receiver's delight and pleasure in using it—and thinking of us when they do so.

Such is the gift of the Spirit of Christ living in us. God wants us to use it, enjoy it, and find pleasure in it. We're to use it every day. The Spirit of Christ in us never loses its color, never wears out.

Where will you use the gift of Christ living in you today?

Thursday • When you use the gift of Christ living in you, it is a miraculous thing. It is supernatural. In your daily life, it might not feel supernatural, but it is. Recently I was telling a physician friend about a physical problem I was having. She indicated the exercise I was doing was not enough, and said she would get me a pamphlet on some other exercises. I was irritated at her suggestion. After all, I was pretty proud of what I was doing and expected her support. My voice reflected my irritation and ended the conversation. Later that afternoon I phoned her and apologized for my tone and shortness. Of course that interaction is not miraculous in the ways we sometimes think of miraculous, but in some ways for me it was. I have trouble admitting I am wrong and apologizing. I can rationalize any position pretty effectively in my head. Christ living in me moves me to hear myself, to take that step, to make some shift.

What difference will occur in your day because Christ is living in you? With your spouse, with your children, with a coworker?

Friday • The fruits of the Spirit named by Saint Paul in his Letter to the Galatians are love, joy, peace, patience, kindness, goodness, faithfulness, gentleness, and self-control. All these fruits are right here in our lives. They are here to help us live as disciples of Christ, to turn the world—our own little or not-so-little everyday world—upside down.

Sometimes I confuse the fruits of the Spirit and the gifts of the Spirit. When I consider the fruits mentioned above, it helps to consider them as a fruit, such as a banana or a pear. I may have those fruits on my counter, but they take time to ripen, to be at their finest. The fruits of the Spirit have to ripen also. I need the Holy Spirit living within me to bring love, joy, peace, patience, kindness, goodness, faithfulness, gentleness, and self-control to their fullest flavor in my life—to come to "fruition."

My friend Karen, who has been involved in our state's recovery from tropical storm Irene, taps into these gifts every day. Her efforts immediately following the devastation of the storm were herculean: picking up huge donations, making certain they got to the right agencies and centers and victims, then daily phoning, coordinating, and following up. Even months later she continued to receive donations and distribute them—all while going through another round of chemo. Patience, goodness, faithfulness, gentleness.

Which of these fruits are you tapping into today? Which ones will help you live the redeemed life Christ has promised?

Saturday • Charles Dickens talks of holding on to some of those qualities of being childlike and says that when we do, we preserve a freshness, a gentleness, and a capacity of being pleased. Isn't that a delightful description of someone? Wouldn't you love it if friends described you as having a "freshness, a gentleness, a capacity of being pleased"? That is certainly not someone who lives a defeated life. That is someone who retains the qualities of childhood, who nurtures the fruits of the Spirit, and someone who believes they have been redeemed…redeemed to live the life of discipleship.

Is that you?

Week 22: Courage

All of them were filled with the Holy Spirit and began to speak in other languages, as the Spirit gave them ability. Now there were devout Jews from every nation under heaven living in Jerusalem… and each one heard them speaking in the native language of each.…All were amazed and perplexed, saying to one another, "What does this mean?" But others sneered and said, "They are filled with new wine."–ACTS 2:4–6, 12–13

Sunday • What do we have if we have the Spirit? Certainly power. Another thing is courage. We need courage, don't we? We're afraid—hesitant and timid—to stand up and take risks for the causes of Christ. Instead of speaking, we remain silent. Instead of acting, we hide and do nothing. And that's a tragedy, because the risen Christ is depending on us to get the work done on earth. He is counting on us to continue his mission of bringing God's love and grace to others. He is counting on us to feed the hungry, to comfort the brokenhearted, to support the downtrodden, and to befriend the lonely.

To do all this requires courage; discipleship is not for the faint-hearted. It takes courage to respond when there is a need, to become involved in the messy lives of others, to sacrifice, to forgive, and to keep on giving of yourself until you think there is nothing left. It takes a lot of courage to be a disciple.

And that is exactly what the Spirit gives us. He energizes us. He enables us to take risks, to overcome our fears, to go the extra mile, to stand up for Christ in the face of ridicule and rejection. He gives us the courage to be fools for Christ!

Monday • When I think of courage, I'm reminded of the book *Undaunted Courage*, the story of Lewis and Clark and their expedition to the Northwest where no white people had ever traveled. The adventures of Lewis and Clark make for a fascinating story of entering unknown land and uncharted waters, meeting obstacles and people whose responses were unpredictable at best, humiliating and life-threatening at worst.

Isn't that the kind of courage needed for discipleship? We don't have a map. We enter unfamiliar territory, and we can't plan for how people might react to this message of love and grace. The Scripture reading tells us the people who heard the Apostles "speak in other languages" were "amazed and perplexed." People who hear our message of love and grace may also be "amazed and perplexed." This message may be so unfamiliar in our culture, it's almost as if we are speaking in a different language.

What message of love and grace will you give today that will leave listeners "amazed and perplexed"?

Tuesday • It is reasonably comfortable to give a message of love and grace within a group of like-minded people. However in today's culture of disbelief, politics, and ridicule, it can be intimidating to give that message clearly to a broader audience.

In the 2011 football season, one star of the game received significant criticism for his use of prayer during parts of each football game he played. Media and newspapers were full of discussions of the "appropriateness" of his gestures. He was both ridiculed and supported. Though I'm reminded of the psalm (147:10) that says God's "delight is not in the strength of the horse nor…the speed of a runner"—Old Testament sports—I do take note of the player's courage to take the message of his faith into the public arena. At least the conversation moved from drugs and steroids and bad behavior to the "appropriateness" of a message of faith. People started to talk about the effectiveness of prayer.

Do you have a message of faith you would like to share with a broader audience? Do you have the courage to speak it? Today?

Wednesday • The familiar Serenity Prayer also speaks to us of courage. "God grant me the serenity to accept the things I cannot change, the courage to change the things I can, and the wisdom to know the difference." In the recovery community, the things I cannot change are usually referred to as other "people, places, and things." Very true, especially people. So many times I hear myself saying, "If only he or she would do this…or stop that…or change that." This is not going to happen just because I want change!

Instead, I concentrate on the "courage to change the things I can." Not only can we change things about ourselves, such as our behaviors and our attitudes, but we can change the world. Yes, little by little we can change our world. Christ asks us to turn our world upside down. It's easy to cop out and say "they" are responsible for their own lives. It's easy to say to the relapsing friend, "You've got to want it." It's easy to say to the housebound elderly woman, "You'll have to find someone else…I'm too busy."

Discipleship is not for the faint-hearted, and it's not for the "too busy." The risen Christ gives us the courage to stop the merry-go-round, get off, and enter the world.

What step off the merry-go-round and into the world of messy lives and sacrifice will you take today?

Thursday • Unfortunately on several occasions, it has been said of me, "She's had too much wine." And even more unfortunately, it was not said because I was sharing God's message of love and grace as were the Apostles. It was because I had had too much wine. Period!

It is not only in the public areas of our lives that we need the courage God has given us through the Holy Spirit. It is so often in our own lives that we need that courage. Folks who are in recovery from addiction can be challenged on a daily basis to make that right decision, that loving decision. They can decide to not pick up that drink or drug, to not call that dealer, to not go to the casino, to not go to the shopping network.

It takes courage to live a life of love and grace.

Feel that courage within you today—the courage God has given you through the Holy Spirit to make the loving decisions in your own life.

Friday • If you speak up as a disciple, what is it that you fear? One of the areas we could each make a difference in is the area of prejudice. Prejudice starts in our homes, in our neighborhoods, in our schools, at our places of work. I remember a Supreme Court Justice candidate saying at a congressional hearing, "In my home I never heard one word of prejudice. It simply was not even a consideration in my parents' house." How often in today's world and even in our homes and social settings do we hear a racial joke? Do we speak up and say, "That's not permitted here" or "I find that offensive"? Or do we smile even in our discomfort and fear being ridiculed if we protest? Not saying something gives assent to prejudice and bullying.

Are you afraid to speak up when you hear something offensive and denigrating to others? Or do you find the courage because you are a disciple of Christ?

Saturday • I would guess that Lewis and Clark had some serious moments of doubt in their adventure into the uncharted Northwest as they confronted all the obstacles in their exploration. I would guess that many of us in recovery from addiction and other demons have some serious moments of doubt about being able to travel this road of recovery with its struggles and challenges. And I would guess all of us have moments of doubt as to whether we have the courage to follow this road of discipleship. One theologian writes that the path of discipleship is narrow with an abyss on both sides. It is only by keeping our eyes on the risen Christ and going step by courageous step that we make our way.

Is there a small courageous step you can take today on your way of discipleship? What is that step?

Week 23: JOY

Therefore my heart was glad and my tongue rejoiced; moreover my flesh will live in hope. For you will not abandon my soul to Hades....You have made known to me the ways of life.

—ACTS 2:26–28

Sunday • Not only do we have power and courage when we have the Spirit, we also have joy: "My tongue rejoiced." Don't confuse joy with happiness. Happiness is dependent on outward circumstances. If the sky is blue and free of dark clouds, then I'm happy. If the sky darkens, gloom sets in.

Joy is much more substantial than a shallow happiness that disappears with an adverse change in circumstances. For the disciple of Christ, joy is believing that our sins have been washed away forever. Joy is the assurance that because of the Spirit, the risen Christ is not only with us but he is within us; he dwells in our hearts. Joy is realizing that Christ has made us part of his mission and work; that he has entrusted us to finish what he started. Joy is the certainty that we can wake up in the morning and know that we are the beloved children of God no matter what comes our way this day.

Monday • When I first heard that happiness was "superficial," I was rather offended. After all, happiness is a feeling I work hard to obtain. I work hard to keep my kids happy, to portray a happy, confident presence, to keep employees happy. But that is all it is—a feeling. Happiness is something I can create by something I do either for myself or for others. And unhappiness is also something I can create for myself or others by a decision or an attitude. Unhappiness is the gloom of a dark sky or the gloom created by poor decisions, a poor attitude, broken relationships, or bad behavior. Gloom is dreary.

Think about the times you feel happy. What is going on in your life? What has caused you to feel happy? Is it something you have done? Is it something someone else has done for you? Happiness is a delightful feeling.

Consider the times in your life when you have been most unhappy. What was going on? Something you did? Something someone else did? Gloom is the absence of joy.

Do you consider yourself happy at this time in your life? What creates that happiness? Will it stay forever, or does it depend on something that can disappear?

Tuesday • Joy is something quite different than happiness. The Sunday devotion says joy is *substantial*. Sometimes joy is portrayed as exuberant, shouting and running and waving one's arms, like a soccer player after scoring a goal. But that is happiness. It can disappear in a minute when the other team scores. Joy, on the other hand, is lasting. It is deep and profound. There is a sense of celebration of something deep within. Gospel music is often called a "joyful noise." "Clap your hands, all you peoples: shout to God with loud songs of joy" (Psalm 47:1). Why? Because it is a deep, profound exclamation of a belief in God's goodness, a belief in God's presence in our lives—even when those lives are challenged and messy.

What times in your life have you felt joy? Has it been a time you sensed the "everlasting joy" of God's presence in your life?

Today consider the moments you feel happy…consider the moments of joy. Is there a difference?

Wednesday • Joy has many attributes, but one thing we recognize in joy is that it fills us completely. It is peaceful; it calms us. Joy is fresh and new, bright and clear. When we feel joy, nothing can touch us. Nothing can bother us or annoy us. Joy covers us and yet shines through us. "God has gone up with a shout, the LORD with the sound of a trumpet" (Psalm 47:5). Joy is Easter morning with trumpets blaring, announcing Christ's resurrection, our redemption.

Joy is knowing our sins are forgiven—forever. Whatever it was that offended God, that caused loved ones pain, God has forgiven us. Joy is faith in God's love. Others can see this joy and this faith.

Will others see joy in you today? Will they sense that joy is because of God's love?

Thursday • Joy is also strength…strength to go ahead and engage in God's work here on earth. Whom do you think of when you consider the strength of doing God's work based in joy? One person who comes to mind is Blessed Teresa of Calcutta. She was a quiet nun who provided care to thousands and thousands of sick and destitute people in India. Through her quiet strength and faith, she developed hospitals and places of care where the most impoverished ill are treated with care and love. Pictures of her reflect a deep, quiet joy.

Few of us are going to rise to the level of this diminutive woman, but each of us, in our daily lives, can reflect a strength that comes from the joy we feel of the risen Christ within us. Christ is not "out there" watching us from afar. He is here within us, giving us the strength to do the loving thing, to be involved in his work.

What work of Christ's is yours to do today?

Friday • We are not just to meditate on Christ's thoughts and words. We are not just to think and analyze and talk about Christ's work here on earth. We are not just to be keepers of the Law. We are not just to meet our obligations. We are to be involved, to continue his work, not watch from the sidelines.

Sometimes that means we have work to do in our personal lives. It means acknowledging the behavior or thoughts that move us away from God, and it means doing something about them. It means changing something, taking some action that commits us to a different path. There is joy in those decisions. There is joy in the freedom those changes produce. There is relief and a flooding of peace. There is the abundant life Christ promises.

Sometimes that work means becoming involved with others—maybe even involved in a way that is uncomfortable. It might mean visiting the elderly in a nursing home, volunteering at a homeless shelter, mentoring a troubled child. It might mean giving up some of our precious free time.

Joy comes when we "get on with it."

What change in your behavior might you commit to today? Can you think of the relief you would feel when that disturbing behavior is gone or when you commit to involvement with others in a way that furthers Christ's work? Can you quit thinking about it and "get on with it"?

Saturday • Joy fills the God-shaped void. We know joy when we believe we are the beloved sons and daughters of God. We sense God is with us and in us. We sense his protection. We sense his strength. We take the risk. We get involved. We face our demons, our greed, our lying, our addictions, and we are able to say, "No more!" We sense his power and we take action. We are not victims. We are the conquerors Saint Paul tells us we are.

We keep this joy alive by prayers many times a day. We ask

God to remind us that he is right here to give his strength to make the right decision. We keep this joy alive with frequent reception of the sacraments. He is right here. Dance, smile, sing—you are alive! You are God's cherished child.

Have you given yourself permission to experience this deep joy?

Week 24: Protection

It is that very Spirit bearing witness with our spirit that we are children of God.–ROMANS 8:16

Sunday • We hear a lot about identity theft these days, but when we live in the Spirit, we have "identity protection." Identity protection intervenes for us from the forces around us and within us that make every effort to rob us of our identity. The guilt that floods us when we have done something wrong, the regrets that overwhelm us when we review our lives, the weaknesses that constantly trip us up, the inadequacies that often make us look like fools—all these things have a way of threatening our identity.

But the Spirit will not allow that; the Spirit will not allow the guilt within us or the world around us to define who we are. There is no need for us to think of ourselves or present ourselves as worthless, miserable failures who have no right to take up space on the earth. The Spirit says otherwise. Consider the words of Saint Paul: The Spirit himself bears witness with our spirit that we are God's children. Listen to the Spirit as he whispers in your ear: You are God's precious child. God has redeemed you and made you his own. You have infinite worth. Listen to the Spirit and walk with your head held high.

Monday • When our identity is stolen through credit cards or bank statements or online accounts, it's a mess. It takes incredible paperwork and phone calls to clarify who we really are and often to reestablish our credit. And then, just in case it might happen to us again, we have to spend money to buy identity protection. Advertisements tell us that terrible things can happen when our identity is stolen. And in our very consumer-focused culture, that is true.

But that is not how it is with God. He knows who we are, and he never forgets. As my favorite Psalm 139 says, "My frame was not hidden from you, when I was being made in secret" (15). God has known who we are from the very beginning: "You know when I sit down and when I rise up....Even before a word is on my tongue, O Lord, you know it completely" (2, 4). God knows our identity forever and ever. It can never be stolen from him. Next time you hear a commercial or see an advertisement about identity theft, remember, "O Lord... you search out my path and my lying down, and are acquainted with all my ways" (3).

Do you worry that God doesn't know who you are? Remind yourself today that he has known you from the beginning.

Tuesday • Who tells you who you are? As we have said before, our self-image, our identity, is crucial to how we respond to life. This identity often determines whether we take advantage of opportunities, whether we take risks that move us to better jobs or new relationships. If our early messages have been "you can do it," we are much more apt to try new things. If messages about our worth have been more negative, we may remain stuck in tired, unsatisfying, even abusive situations.

At this point in your life, who tells you who you are? Who or what gives you your identity? Is it your house, the car you drive, your clothes, your job? Is it your past decisions, the choices you have made, both good and bad? Do you spend any time thinking of your spiritual identity? Could someone steal that from you? What is your spiritual-identity protection?

Who do you say you are spiritually? If someone were to ask, "What do you believe?" what would you say?

Wednesday • Having worked professionally in the field of addiction and recovery for many years and having been challenged by the disease myself, I am very aware of relapse as an ongoing struggle for many people. (Of course, relapse is not only part of addiction but also part of the many demons that challenge us in our lives.) A recent journal article gave statistics on the recovery rate for physicians who were in a monitored recovery program. The recovery rates without relapse were incredibly high. As I thought about those rates, I thought of the self-image, the identity, the self-esteem of physicians and what they have to lose if they relapse. If they are successful in their recovery, they return to a high-paying profession, probably to families who care about them, a protective community. Their "winner" identity remains intact.

Not so for many people who struggle for recovery. Often they have no job, no family, no transportation, no housing, and a probation officer expecting them to fail. Their identity, their self-image, is one of "loser."

If you were to relapse into one of your demons, do you have a supportive person or community? Do you turn back to God, to the one relationship that never turns you away, who fills you with the power to succeed, who knows who you are?

Thursday • When I was working as a nurse manager on a substance-abuse unit, it was not unusual to have recovering people on staff. After all, those of us in recovery have life experience that we hope will be useful in our professional roles.

It's part of our identity. One of the nurses I was working with had had several recent car accidents and requested time off. I was reporting on staffing at a management meeting, and the supervisor asked, "Is something else going on here?" My reply was, "Well, I don't know. She is an alcoholic." Another manager spoke right up and said, "I wish you had said she is in recovery from alcoholism."

Now there is a difference in identity! What a shift in others' immediate perception of her and the situation. Since that moment I have always tried to be specific. No one is a disease or a demon. What we call ourselves, or others, is very important.

How would you describe yourself to God today? Do you acknowledge he knows you in all ways?

Friday • When people used to call themselves by their professions, we knew what Sam Carpenter did or John Wheelright or Charles Fisher or Abe Brickman. In some cultures, Johnson or Davidson told people who their fathers were. Surnames often give a sense of who they "belonged" to.

As a new bride, I remember being a bit surprised when I used my new name. My identity had changed, and it now meant I "belonged" to my husband and his family. I was no longer my father's daughter. Many women still wonder by what name they call themselves after marriage.

The Scripture reading for this week says that the Spirit himself bears witness that we are God's children. Here again is a legal word that claims who we are...who we "belong to." In a court of law, God's court, the Spirit says we are God's children—no qualifiers, no restrictions, forever.

Do you hear the forever promise, the sworn oath in God's covenant, that you are God's child?

Saturday • Have you changed your name? My niece Polly is now Paula. My grandson Jake is now his given name Jack. What other name do you go by? Do you go by the name Christian? Where did you receive that name? You received it in baptism. As I've said before, I love it when a baptism takes place at Sunday Mass and the priest turns with the child in his arms and says to the congregation, "Please welcome the newest Christian." Or when an adult is baptized and a smile spreads across his or her face.

Today as you consider your many roles or titles, can you put "Christian" in front of them? I am a "Christian parent...a Christian spouse...a Christian lawyer...a Christian teacher...a Christian secretary...a Christian truckdriver...a Christian_____." Does that make a difference? The Spirit gives you the power.

Does it make you hold your head high? Do you walk taller because of that identity? Do you smile?

What if "Christian" is not how you identify yourself? What difference would it make in your life if that was part of your identity? What if it were your *primary* identity?

Week 25: Live...

...you who have received the Spirit.–GALATIANS 6:1

Sunday • In his Letter to the Galatians, Saint Paul talks about a "spiritual person" and then throughout Galatians as well as his Letter to the Romans, he describes what a spiritual person is.

The first thing Saint Paul says is that a spiritual person is someone who *lives* in the Spirit. To live in the Spirit is to rely on the Spirit—to live the life of discipleship. It means to depend on the Spirit's power and presence for the energy as well as the motivation to engage in the service of those who are broken and weary and lonely. It means to trust the Spirit to provide the strength and courage to live a life of faith. It means that we count on the Spirit to renew us as we seek to minister to our spouses and children and neighbors and friends and coworkers.

In spite of what we sometimes think, we don't renew ourselves. We cannot live the Christian life on our own power, we cannot depend on our own resources and abilities to do the work of God, we cannot rely on our own energy and willpower to be the people God redeemed us to be.

And we don't have to. He gives us his Spirit; he is our inspiration; he is the one who wants to renew us day after day. The spiritual person knows this and constantly prays for an outpouring of the Spirit. It's a prayer God loves to answer.

Monday • Over the last couple of years I have been included in the e-mail lists of several friends whose spouses or children are undergoing serious health problems. These e-mail messages are an efficient way of keeping friends and family updated of the progress of a person we care about. For the last several weeks a friend's husband has been undergoing very difficult surgery and rehab. The news has not all been positive. Last week my friend needed to be away from the hospital to lead a workshop as part of her ongoing job. She posted a note to this e-mail list that while she was gone for several days, she needed help from friends to visit her husband, relay information to others, and generally be on standby. The response was overwhelming. Lots of people were available. She could rely on them, depend on them, and trust they would follow through.

We are all aware of times like this when we have to call on others to help us—people we can rely on, depend on, and trust. Do we feel the same way about the Spirit? Do we know we can rely on, depend on, and trust that the Spirit will respond when we call?

What do you need today from the Spirit to live a life of discipleship? Do you absolutely trust the Spirit is there for you?

Tuesday • The Sunday devotion says we need faith to live a life of discipleship. I love the saying from Hebrews 11 that says faith is the confident assurance concerning what we hope for and conviction about things we do not see. When we pray to the Spirit for confident assurance to live a life of discipleship, to do or say something that is uncomfortable or even frightening, we do not necessarily see or feel an infusion of strength or courage, but we hope and trust it will be there. Just as my friend trusted that her friends would respond to her call for help, we can trust that the Spirit will be with us. In faith, we have confident assurance of what we hope for...pray for.

What if your faith is a little shaky? What if you are not real confident, not real trusting, that the strength and courage will be there? You remain open. You pay attention. You listen for God's whisper. You ask for help. You do the loving thing and watch what happens.

Do one unexpected, loving thing today and watch what happens.

Wednesday • A friend who has been challenged with addiction for many years called the other day. She has had long periods of recovery, only for the tiger to bite her again time after time. One of her struggles is that in the past, the craving did not leave. Even after months and months of not using, of praying for the craving to be taken away, she would say, "I still dream about it, still think about it daily." But in the recent phone call, she said, "I am amazed, I haven't even had a craving for weeks. I just can't believe it. I still think about it, but not with a desire; it's more with relief that I don't have to do that anymore." Then with a laugh, she said, "After all these years of praying for God to take away my craving, do you think he has finally answered?" You think?

The life she was redeemed for. "Faith is the assurance of things hoped for and trust in things we cannot see." You think?

Is there something you pray for, something you really need help with to live the life you have been redeemed for? Do you trust that the Spirit is with you in it?

Thursday • Do you see yourself as a spiritual person living the life of discipleship? I would guess that very few of us would identify ourselves in that way. But look at your day—who do you interact with? How do you relate to them? Do you reflect God's love in your time with your spouse and children? Do you reflect that faith in your interactions at work and with your congregation? (Sometimes I am amused and saddened at how little ministry we experience with one another at church as we argue over committees, money, and liturgy!) Do you call those interactions "ministry"?

It is all an opportunity for ministry. It is all an opportunity to live a life of discipleship.

Today, watch the interactions around you. Who shows gentleness, patience, and self-control—all those fruits of the Spirit that help us live a life of discipleship? Do you?

Friday • To live a life of discipleship sounds challenging. A person could get worn out trying to always be ministering!

But like my friend who put out the call for help with her sick husband, we do not need to do it alone. One thing to note is that my friend did not all of a sudden ask for help. She had kept us up-to-date on what her husband's situation was, where and when she might need help. We need to do the same thing with our prayers for help to lead a life of discipleship. God loves to be in the loop, on our e-mail list about what's going on in our lives. Our relationship with God is sustained in our prayer life. He is always there. He has given us the fruits of the Spirit to sustain us, to renew us.

We have the help, if only we will use it, call on it—love, joy, patience, peace, kindness, goodness, faithfulness, gentleness, and self-control.

Which fruit of the Spirit might you need most today? Can you remember to call on it?

Saturday • Have you ever had the experience of deciding not to renew a subscription to a magazine, only to have the renewal cost appear on your credit card bill? So you call the magazine, and they announce that it's an "automatic renewal." You tell them to take it off your bill, that you don't want the magazine anymore. Well, that is real frustrating with a magazine subscription, but that "automatic renewal" is the good news with the Spirit's presence in our lives. It's always there—always replenished. You just need to remind yourself it is there—always there—so use it.

Which fruit of the Spirit do you use most frequently? Does it sometimes feel like it runs out? Do you pray to be reminded of its renewal? It is there—always.

Week 26: Walk...

...you who have received the Spirit. –GALATIANS 6:1

Sunday • A spiritual person not only lives in the Spirit, but such a person also *walks* in the Spirit. To walk in the Spirit is to be controlled by the Spirit.

What makes this so difficult is that we are often tempted to think we control our own lives. *We* want to call the shots, *we* want to order our lives; we don't want to live under anybody's control. We like to think we are in charge.

When we operate that way, we end up prisoners of our own desires and wants. We end up living a life of self-gratification. That's what the prodigal son did in the parable Jesus told. The prodigal son was no longer able to celebrate life but instead ended up eating with the pigs.

God, however, has not redeemed us to exist in pigpens. He has something much better in mind for us—a life that is really worth living. And those who experience this life are those who walk in the Spirit—those who turn the control of their lives over to the Spirit, those who allow the Spirit to gently lead them in the direction of God. That is the adventure in discipleship!

Monday • I walk daily. It's a beautiful two-mile walk over a mountain, across a rushing brook, down to a large pond, and back. It's steep in places, and I find it very good exercise. In several places the road drops off severely. In winter when it's icy, I pay close attention to where I step.

I walk by myself because I love the quiet and solitude. Only two or three cars go by in a forty-five–minute walk. No cell-phone calls, no iPod; just quiet. Friends question what would happen if I had an "incident" and was alone, but that's a risk I'm willing to take. I don't feel alone. I carry myself with me… thoughts, questions, memories, plans, and prayers.

The Holy Spirit is with me. "The Creator, who made all things," is never more present than in the snow in the woods, the changing color of the trees in the seasons, the flutelike sounds of the scarlet tanagers calling to one another. To walk in the Spirit is to know the Creator controls all things. I couldn't be happier to know this control.

Where do you walk with the Spirit?

Tuesday • It's so easy to think we have control over all of our lives. We think *we* create the opportunities. We think *we* make the decisions. If we take the time to think it all through, we realize that when we open ourselves to the Spirit in our lives, it all becomes so much simpler, so much clearer. When we open ourselves to "love one another," it all becomes less complicated. The prodigal son thought he was in charge. He chose to go to a far-off country. When he really fouled that "freedom" up, when he came to the reality that he had no control over his life, he returned to the open, loving arms of his father. His father was at the end of the road looking for him!

God wants us to celebrate life, to enjoy all that he has created. He does not want us to feel like prisoners in his house. He gives us freedom. He creates a path of beauty and opportunity. We have choices along that path.

Does your life feel like a life God created? Is the Spirit alive in your life? Is God out looking for you?

Wednesday • Many spiritual writers tell us the path to discipleship, the one we must take to be followers of Christ, is narrow. They tell us it is easy to misstep and fall off. We could so easily fall into an abyss of self-importance, conceit, pride, vanity, or arrogance. It's tempting to think we are the ones creating all the good work. We think we have control.

The doers, the real disciples of Christ, build their lives and their works on the grace of God. They are humble people. They acknowledge their own frailties, their own human condition. They have an inner calmness, a strength, a courage that speaks for them.

Do you know someone you consider a disciple of Christ? What qualities do you most admire in them? Would you want more of that?

Thursday • When we make a conscious decision to take the path of discipleship, to open ourselves to the control of our lives by the Spirit, it very well might mean taking a different path. That different path might be a different physical path, and it might also mean a different spiritual path. Ultimately it will mean a path to a life worth living—a life of generosity, lavishness, and abundance. Through the Holy Spirit, God gets us ready for the business of life and living. He prepares us with courage and a certainty of faith.

When we accept our identity as Christians, as sons and daughters of God, we have both privilege and responsibility. We have the privilege and the responsibility to change. The Christian message is that we do not need to stay the way we are. Isn't that amazing? When we walk in the Spirit, we make all decisions within the framework of the life for which God redeemed us. That is giving the control of our lives to the Holy Spirit.

Is there a change in your life that would lead you closer to the path of discipleship? What would that change be? Perhaps it would be a physical change such as a job or a spiritual change such as more attention to prayer, a physical change such as time with your family or a spiritual change such as generosity.

Friday • What keeps you from making the change you identified yesterday? Are you afraid? If so, of what? What is the worst thing that could happen if you made that change? What is the best thing that could happen?

If we are afraid, if we are anxious all the time, we cannot clearly see Christ. Sometimes our anxiety gives us the impression we exist. When we ask people, "How are you?" and their response is a list of how busy they are, they are telling us they exist, they are important. They think they are in control of their lives.

How much freer we might be if we walked in the Holy Spirit, how much less tension, how much more healing of ourselves and others.

What makes you most anxious? How can you recognize the strength of the Holy Spirit that is with you in that anxiety? How can you recognize the Spirit's control today?

Saturday • I spend a great deal of time planning in my head. I plan for good things and bad things. I spend so much time planning that I sometimes miss today. As I have said before, when I find myself doing this, I try to remember about the Israelites in the desert. They were most unhappy with their plight and raised their voices at Moses and God. They said they were following God but didn't even have enough to eat. God answered their prayers and gave them manna, but he only gave them enough for each day. He didn't give them enough to store up for the next day or the week.

I need to remember to focus on today and to remember that God will give me enough for today; all the planning in the world will not change what I project for next week or next month. Of course, some planning is necessary, but for the important things, the things that make a difference in my relationship with God, he will give me enough for today. No matter how hard today seems when I get up in the morning, no matter what difficult situation I must face, the Spirit will give me the strength and the courage...for today.

Today, how will you know the Holy Spirit is walking with you and will give you what you need? How will you know you're not the one in control? Do you sense the abundance, the lavishness of your life?

Week 27 : Be Led...

...you who have received the Spirit.–GALATIANS 6:1

Sunday • We've been looking closely at who is a spiritual person. We've discovered that a spiritual person *lives* in the Spirit, *walks* in the Spirit, and now one who is *led* by the Spirit. To be led by the Spirit means we make plans and decisions based on the Spirit's guidance. To be led by the Spirit is to operate with the underlying principle: I do not belong to myself; rather, because of the life, death, and resurrection of Jesus Christ, I belong to God. I am his! To be led by the Spirit is to be always conscious of his primary concern—that God's will be accomplished in my life.

And that's tough. "Self-will run riot" is what the *Big Book* of Alcoholics Anonymous calls it. That is not only a problem for the addict; it is also a problem for every man and woman. We are tempted to live somewhat in opposition to God. We think it's OK for him to make suggestions about how we are to live, but there are certain areas of our lives that are restricted. We don't feel it's any of his business regarding what we do with our money or sex or business methods. It's no wonder we often end up with such twisted lives.

And it's all so unnecessary. When God invites us to live according to his will, he is not offering us a life of slavery; he is offering us freedom. To be led by the Spirit is to experience a life of joy and purpose and peace. It is the good life.

Monday • So we can plan! We can plan for our education, our job, our family, a vacation. The difference in a life led by the Spirit is to first consider our life, our decisions, in the context of God's will. This is a new way of thinking. It is a new beginning. It is a major shift. It is a different way of shaping our decisions.

Too often we place God's will way down in our decision-making process. Too often only after long-term agonizing and stressing over a decision do we finally remember to consider God's will. Too often, our first consideration in a decision is "What's in it for me?" or "How will this make my life easier?" or "How will this make me feel better?"

When we are able to make this shift to consideration of God's will first, it changes the conversation in our head. It changes our priorities. We enter the process of making the decision with more patience, kindness, gentleness, and faithfulness. The anxiety lessens and we make room for God's will.

Think of a decision you recently made. What was your first priority? Would the process of making the decision have been different if God's will had been your first consideration? Would the ultimate decision have been different?

Tuesday • A popular movie a few years back made the concept of writing a "bucket list," a list of things we want to do before we die, a topic of social conversations. People now talk of what's first on their bucket list or what they've accomplished on their bucket list. It can be places they wish to visit or things they want to do: visit Machu Picchu or go to spring training or walk the Appalachian Trail.

I have never heard anyone say his or her bucket list includes a life led by God. I've heard people say they want to lead a simpler life. They want to get out of the rat race. They want to do volunteer work. They want to do philanthropy. But it's always later. It's not now. It's when I make more money. It's when I do all the traveling I want to do. It's when the kids are gone.

What if today we put at the top of our bucket list that we want to experience a life led by God? Right now. What might that look like?

Wednesday • We can get real possessive of the decisions we make. We can become very self-righteous. "No one is going to tell me how to spend my money. If I want a bigger boat, I earned the money. I can spend it any way I want. I give my pledge on Sunday." Or "I'm just having a little flirtation. It doesn't mean I'm unfaithful to my husband. It just means I'm having a little fun." How many affairs and destroyed marriages have evolved from an "innocent" flirtation, an "innocent" flirtation that niggled at our conscience from the very beginning?

We close down. We shut our minds and our thoughts to consideration of the Spirit. It's our life, we think, and we are in charge! How much easier those decisions would be if we first prayed for God's will and were willing to be led by the Spirit.

Is there a decision today that would be better considered with an openness to God's will for you? Is there someone in your life considering a big decision? Would it be helpful if you mentioned that he or she consider being led by God's will? Can you do that? Do you use the power given to the disciples and you at Pentecost to speak in words that can be heard, that can lead to Christ?

Thursday • How do we do this? How do we open ourselves to be led by the Spirit? It takes prayerful practice. As we said, it is a new beginning, and like any new exercise or regime, it takes practice. We don't learn to ski or play tennis or play bridge the first time out. We practice, practice, practice. We pray to be open to the Spirit.

When we learn a new sport, we get the right equipment, find the right place, get a good teacher. When we learn to pray, we read the words of Scripture. We meditate on those words. We consider what those words mean in our lives today. We pray quietly. We find a place where we sense God's presence. Maybe that would be in a church already sanctified or maybe in a quiet place of nature. Maybe it's in our room, maybe it's in a jail cell. We get the right teacher. We give thought and debate and discussion to our decision always within the context of God's will. And then we trust that God will lead us to a decision. We don't wait for a sign. Waiting for a sign negates our trust in the Spirit's presence. Waiting for a sign leads to magical thinking, and there is no magic in the Spirit's presence.

We pray. We are open. We listen.

How will you practice today to being led by the Spirit? What new effort will you make to be open?

Friday • How will you know which way the Spirit is leading you? If there is no sign, which road do you take? It probably won't be the easier path. It probably won't be the one with more stuff or more money or more prestige. It will be the one that fills the void. It will be the one that calms the anxiety. It will be the one that emerges from a deep place in your soul.

And what if you choose the other path? You know, the one that seems more fun, the one that feels like it's your decision. And what if it becomes clear later that the decision was not the one led by the Spirit? What if your life becomes more stressed, more filled with chaos, more painful? The joy is that you can always re-decide. Maybe you wind up stuck in a contract or a place that only causes distress in some far-off land.

You can always go home again. You are God's child. You belong to that loving God who is waiting for you with open arms.

Are you stuck someplace because of a decision not led by the Spirit? Today can you begin the journey back? Can you begin to pray, to be open, to listen to new guidance from the Spirit?

Saturday • Sometimes the outcome of a decision that seems led by the Spirit turns out to be something entirely different than the outcome we expected. My husband and I moved to

Vermont because living here was on our bucket list. We also were searching for an active congregational life, a life that would nourish us spiritually. As it turns out, Vermont is as beautiful as we imagined. The mountains and the snow remind us daily of God's gift of creation. However a strong spiritual congregation seems to evade us. New Englanders don't like to talk about their beliefs and their spirituality. It's a private thing. So we started our own morning meditation. We read Scripture. We discuss the reading. What might it mean for us in our lives and today? We read a few pages from a favorite spiritual author—maybe Henri Nouwen or Elizabeth Johnson or Joan Chittister or Dietrich Bonhoeffer or Thomas Merton. My husband teaches three Bible classes in two different churches. Attendance is good. People are hungry to hear the Word of God—to find its meaning in their lives—to be led.

It's a different kind of spirituality than we expected, but one clearly led by God.

In your life today, where can you find the Spirit?

Week 28: Be Filled...

...with the Spirit.—EPHESIANS 5:18

Sunday • Finally, a spiritual person is one whose life is *filled* with the Spirit. Do you remember the story Jesus told about the owner of a house who swept his dwelling clean of an evil spirit who had taken up residence in the place? The problem was that the owners left the house empty, and so the evil spirit returned with seven of his friends and they moved in. The owner left a void and missed the point of the Christian life.

So many of us think of the Christian life as a lifelong house-cleaning. We think being a disciple of Christ means making sure the house is without mess or junk. We think it's simply a matter of keeping evil off the doorstep. Now, there is nothing wrong with simplifying. Yet an empty life is dangerous; it needs to be filled with something.

A person can be filled with a lot of different things: alcohol, food, pride, grudges, anger, power, hate, prejudice, greed, lust, anxiety, status, and success. The point is, whatever we are filled with takes over our lives.

God wants us to be filled with his Spirit. When we are filled with the Spirit, Jesus Christ becomes our center, our love. Jesus Christ becomes our life. That's what happened to the Apostle Paul. He said, "For to me, living is Christ" (Philippians 1:21). And in another place he said, "It is no longer I who live, but it is Christ who lives in me" (Galatians 2:20). And that's how it can be for us. That's what God wants for us. He wants to fill us to the brim with the Spirit. That is a life worth living!

Monday • We have a friend in a rural Midwestern state who is the CEO of a large regional hospital. He answers to his Board, and his bottom line must somehow stay solvent in this very difficult time for health care. He has to have adequate staffing to care for the patients, and he has to pay that staff a fair wage and provide benefits. He has to cover the costs of the upkeep of a large, aging building—heat, air conditioning, and plumbing. He has to meet standards of various agencies. Those agency reviews cost staff time. He must pay for new costly equipment. The emergency room and hospital units must care for persons who have no health insurance.

I asked him how he makes all these difficult decisions. He said, "I pray. I pray that the Spirit will guide me. I try to surround myself with bright people, people who know their part of the process, their unit, their responsibility. We talk. We dialogue. I get the best information I can, and then I pray some more. I pray this is the best decision I can make for the hospital, for the staff, for the people of our community. Those are the people I serve. Then I live with it. If it doesn't work out, if I get criticized, I know I involved the Spirit in the decision, so I go back and ask for further guidance."

This man has a wonderful reputation in the community—a reputation for fairness, for honesty, for gentleness, for compassion, for truth. He is filled with the Spirit in his decisions, in his life.

What is your reputation in the community? Would others say you are filled with the Spirit? Do you think you are filled with the Spirit? How do you know?

Tuesday • We have many, many ways to be filled with the Spirit in our daily lives. When we are driving, we don't respond to someone's driving error with road rage. We smile and give a little wave, knowing we've made that same mistake. If we are renters, we take care of the property. Wouldn't we want someone to take care of our belongings? If we are at a laundromat and someone asks if we have change, we share. We may even make a habit of taking some extra change with us in case someone needs it. If our spouse or children use a sharp tone of voice with us, we don't escalate the issue. We stop, pray for the Spirit, and say to ourselves, *This can stop with me. I can use another tone. I can ask what's going on.*

There are so many ways to have the Spirit fill our daily lives. How will that be for you today?

Wednesday • I have a friend who does such wonderful ministry. She works with hospice, visiting very ill people. She volunteers at her large church doing many small jobs and spreads the gospel through work with a national women's organization. She has elderly friends she takes to lunch weekly.

But she is so angry. Most of her anger centers on her husband of more than twenty years. It seems he can do nothing right. Her anger at him literally consumes her at times. And she seems unable to step away from the anger. She goes to therapy and says it's working, but the anger still fills most of our conversations.

I wonder what her life would be like if she could leave that anger behind. Would it create a void, only to be filled with a different evil spirit? Has anger become such a way of life, so consuming, such a habit, that she can't let it go? Or would she find some peace? Would the Spirit's quiet joy fill the void?

Is there an evil spirit that fills you, something that destroys the peace God wants for you? Today can you pray for the Spirit to help you sweep that evil out of your house?

Thursday • It's easy to forget the Spirit is with us all the time. It's easy to forget the Spirit really does fill us. We often talk of "calling on" the Spirit as though he were out there somewhere. But when we remind ourselves through prayer that he is within us, there is a different sense of how we are to be—of how we are to be with ourselves, with others, and with God.

I notice a difference when I "call on" God when I am sad or frightened. It does feel like he's out there waiting for me to call, but "out there" nonetheless. When I'm living with the Spirit filling my life, I experience a sense of peace, a sense of being on the path, of walking, of being led, a sense that he knows me.

It is good to "call on" the Spirit when I have forgotten he fills me. It's even better to pray for a life filled with the Spirit.

Friday • In my book *Broken by Addiction, Blessed by God*, I tell the story of a woman named Nancy. Nancy is not an educated woman in the sense of higher degrees, but she is certainly educated in the way of life. She is one of the most spiritual women I know. She lives a life filled with the Spirit. She says that when she first experienced her breathing problems, she would say to

God, "Let's just sit here and rest a little." She experiences God in every part of her life. Recently when I told her she was the most spiritual person I know, she said, "Well, I don't have all the knowledge in my head. I just have it in my heart."

That's it! We don't have to have great knowledge and insight; we just have to have great trust in God's love, his promises, his presence. Do you?

Saturday • How do we get there? How do we move to a life filled with the Spirit? We already have it, we just need to recognize it day by day. Each morning is a new beginning. Every day is whole in and of itself. Day and night were created to give us boundaries. God's mercy is new each morning. We come to this new life filled with the Spirit in prayer each morning. We have a right to this quiet time—to this time to ask God to fill us this day. With the Spirit filling us, we do not need to fear the day; we do not need to see the burden of the day. We look to the gifts, to the opportunity, to the newness of our lives—in the middle of our lives.

What new miracle fills your life today? How will you know you walk with the Spirit, are led by the Spirit, and are filled with the Spirit? Today is whole within itself.

Week 29: Words

With it we bless the Lord and Father, and with it we curse those who are made in the likeness of God. From the same mouth come blessing and cursing. My brothers and sisters, this ought not to be so. Does a spring pour forth from the same opening both fresh and brackish water? Can a fig tree, my brothers and sisters, yield olives, or a grapevine figs? No more can salt water yield fresh.—JAMES 3:9–12

Sunday • "Sticks and stones can break my bones, but words can never hurt me."

But that's not true, is it? Words can have a huge effect on us. Words can make us feel good about ourselves, and words can also make us feel miserable and worthless. In his Epistle, Saint James talks about the power of the tongue. He compares it to a small spark that is able to set a great forest on fire. He says that no man can tame the tongue. It is restless and full of deadly poison. There is really no arguing with that. From our own experience, we know how the words of others have hurt us and how our words have hurt others.

So how do we control our tongues? By opening our hearts and lives to the Spirit of Christ. The more the Spirit takes control of us, the more we are empowered to take control of our tongues. The words we use in our daily conversations demonstrate that we are someone in whom the Word, Jesus Christ, lives. So ask yourself, What kind of words am I using regularly? Are they words that express love? Are they words that build up others? Are they words that hurt and wound? Are they words that show care? Are they words that convey forgiveness? James says, "Out of the same mouth come praise and cursing." What comes out of your mouth?

Monday • In the first week of Pentecost, we considered the Scripture verse that described the Holy Spirit descending upon the Apostles in tongues of fire, men who spoke different languages and different dialects were able to understand the Apostles' teachings, each in their own language. That is the power of the Holy Spirit. That is what we sense when we let the Holy Spirit take control of our lives, when we walk, are led, live, and are filled with the Holy Spirit. When we are alive in the Holy Spirit, we speak in a way that is different. We speak in a way that is loving, that builds relationships and community. We speak in a way that people will listen.

We know an older gentleman who complains that nobody listens to him anymore. But when one does listen, all that comes out of his mouth is complaining. He complains about "the dregs of society" he used to work with. He complains about a daughter-in-law who doesn't respect his son. He complains about people in the congregation who don't agree with him on certain issues. People walk away.

The power of the Holy Spirit lets us be heard.

What are the most powerful words you use? How do people respond? Today use a word or phrase of care and concern. Watch how the listener responds.

Tuesday • The power of words is not only in the words themselves but in the tone and gestures we use. As a psychiatric nurse, I have spent much of my professional life listening and talking. I have spent hours helping people examine an experience or incident, what meaning it has for them, what impact it has on their lives, and how they might use those insights for personal growth. A large part of my role in that work is not only to examine the words they use but the way they say them. What is their tone, what gestures do they use? When someone says, "I really don't care," but has sadness in her eyes or tone, that needs to be examined. If our spouse says, "Let's talk about that," but his arms are crossed over his chest, we sense this isn't going to be an easy conversation.

When we live in the Holy Spirit, we pay attention not only to our words but also to our tone and gestures. We are open to exploring the words and tone and gestures of others in our families, in our work, in our congregations. We don't let conversations end abruptly and with misunderstanding. Words are powerful.

Today if you don't thoroughly understand the meaning behind what someone says, do you have the courage to say, "I'm not sure what you mean. Can you say more about that?" Too often what comes off our lips is, "I know," when in fact we *don't* know—we have no idea what that person is experiencing.

Wednesday • Sometimes these days I am appalled at the language I hear. It isn't just in the movies, it's everywhere: when I'm waiting in line at the supermarket, when I'm sitting on the bus and the person behind me is talking on a cell phone, when I'm on a plane or riding the train. Every other word is a swear word. I'm never quite sure what to do. I don't like confrontation, so I'm reluctant to say something. What am I afraid of—that they won't like me? A tongue like that rarely gives blessing. About the best I wind up doing is giving them a disapproving look. What I get in return is, "What are you looking at?"

What do I get out of an interaction like that? I get a reminder that Christ lives in me. I have control over what comes out of my mouth. I don't have control over others.

Thursday • We are empowered by the Holy Spirit to control what comes out of our mouths, and to some extent, what comes out of the mouths of our children and grandchildren. One of the greatest roles we play is that of parents. We teach our children words and tone and gestures to express their feelings in a constructive, loving way. We can role-model, set an example, and set limits on what they say and how they say it. When children are fighting with their brothers and sisters, they can learn to express themselves in ways that are not hurtful. They will use the language they learn from their parents, from their peers, from other adults. As we teach, we can use words, tone, and gestures that not only give boundaries but also give blessing.

Christ set limits as he shared the Good News. He threw the moneychangers out of the Temple. He told the Apostles to let the children come to him, to let the sick approach him. He gave the greatest commandment, "You shall love the Lord your God with all your heart, and with all your soul, and with all your mind." And the second is like it, "You shall love your neighbor as yourself."

Do you use words that model love and caring? Are those the words you hear your children using?

Friday • The stories we tell reveal who we are. Combat pilots tell their stories over and over. It's as though the stories define who they are. Mothers retell the stories of what their children did to anyone who will listen. Sports figures replay the catch or the homerun over and over.

Christ gave the message of the power of the Father's love, the worth of the kingdom, the meaning of justice, all in stories, in parables, in words. Those stories defined who he was and his purpose in life: to redeem us to a life held in God's love. He didn't use gossip. He didn't tell us about the background of the woman found in adultery. He didn't tell us much about the Apostles' background. None of that was important. What was important was that we heard the message of forgiveness and redemption.

What stories do you tell most frequently? Do they define

who you are and what's important in your life? What *is* most important in your life?

Saturday • Hearing the words of Christ, pondering them in our hearts, and working toward finding the meaning of those words in our lives moves us to a spiritual life. It moves us to a gentle life. It moves us with courage to share those words with others. Hearing those words gives us freedom. We discover the freedom to live the lavish life of being forgiven...and to forgive others. Hearing the words of Christ unburdens us from guilt and shame. Hearing the words of Christ empowers us to walk with Christ, to be led by Christ, to live in Christ, to live the life of discipleship.

The tongues of fire came to the disciples so that all could hear the message of Christ. The fire of the Holy Spirit fills us so that those around us can hear the message of Christ.

"The glory of God is in the human being fully alive!"

Are you fully alive? How do you know?

Understanding Jesus:
How Can We Be Apostles?

The next eight weeks consider ways in which the Apostles came to know Christ and to follow him. In what ways do you come to know Christ in your life and to follow him?

Week 30: Storms to Calm

Immediately he made the disciples get into the boat and go on ahead to the other side, while he dismissed the crowds...When evening came, he was there alone, but by this time the boat, battered by the waves, was far from the land, for the wind was against them. And early in the morning he came walking towards them on the lake.–MATTHEW 14:22–25

Sunday • We've all taken this journey. For a while we sail along smoothly under blue skies and across calm waters, and then suddenly, dark and angry clouds fill the skies and a raging storm erupts. We find ourselves in a desperate struggle, losing strength and filled with weariness, frustration, and anxiety.

There are a multitude of things we might be carrying with us in the boat: guilt, shame, regret, declining health, financial troubles, relationship difficulties. At such times we feel alone. What to do?

In the story of the disciples on the Sea of Galilee, we are told that Jesus came to them, walking on the sea. That's the sheer beauty of the Gospel message. It tells us that we are not alone—that across the storms of life, Christ comes to us to be by our side and to steady us and support us and to hold us in his arms. All we need to do is keep our eyes fixed on him.

Monday • We don't need a weather map to know that the storms that blow into our lives are caused by many different circumstances. Sometimes they arise from situations over which we have no control: the economy, job loss, health challenges. But they might come from high-pressure zones we can control: how we spend our money, lifestyle choices, and whom we choose to spend time with. Our life-storms can be sudden and fierce. Sometimes they are so numerous we think we're in the midst of tornadoes and we're losing the strength to deal with them.

Looking at these situations helps us to identify which storms we can control and which ones we cannot. On a visit with a friend I hadn't seen in quite a while, I asked, "So how is your life?" She was able to name each storm, and after some discussion—without any prompting on my part—she identified current situations where she had some choices and where she did not.

What are the storms in your life? Are they clearly identifiable or vague fears? Where do you have some control? Where not? Who promises you support and help?

Tuesday • The big storms in our lives often resurface because of past decisions. The situation we are now in may be new, but the effects of those old decisions may still have an impact. Storms can blow in because of decisions we made when we were at a different place in our lives. Perhaps it was a decision about a job or school or who to marry. Perhaps it was what we decided to eat or drink or who to have sex with. We are "powerless" over our past but not over our current decisions.

What decisions from your past create storms in your present? What small new decision can you make today that would quiet the storm—even if only slightly? From whom does the power to re-decide come?

Wednesday • Some of the storms in our lives feel less like raging seas and more like the premonitions of a storm to come. Either way, we feel threatened. In terms of our feelings, these lesser storms feel like an undercurrent of anxiety. Sometimes we are unable to name or identify that undercurrent. Sometimes we are not even aware of it. However, that feeling of threat or ongoing anxiety is just as exhausting and dangerous as the raging storms.

Ongoing anxieties can spin off and spawn future storms if we choose not to recognize them. They can limit our connections with others. Fears and anxieties can affect our conversations, our relationships, and even our spirituality.

Are there times you feel an anxiety you are not certain you understand? Does it affect who you are with others? Does the anxiety affect your relationship with God? If so, in what way?

Thursday • Where do these stormy undercurrents come from? Often this anxiety has been with us a very long time. We think of it as just the way life is, just the way we are. Even the psalmist from the Old Testament says, "Why are you cast down, O my soul, and why are you disquieted within me?" (42:5).

Anxiety is so uncomfortable, we generally just want it to go away. However, when we pay attention to the times we feel most anxious, we have a chance to identify how it affects our bodies and where it comes from. Our bodies are incredible sources of information. If we pay attention to the tenseness in our neck, the headache, the clenched fists, we get early warnings of building anxieties and stressors—storms on the horizon.

Where in your body does the anxiety show itself? Do you acknowledge it is there—that it is an important message about who you are and where you have come from? Do you remember who gave you the gift of this miraculous body?

Friday • Our anxieties can stem from a current situation, and they can also be expectations we have of ourselves or that others have placed on us. These expectations might have been very well intended as guides to make us "good" people. But they also might have given us a sense that we must perform perfectly and productively at all times. Along the way, we developed the theory that we must be right at all times and we must never show others our vulnerabilities. Those expectations in and of themselves can lead us into creating storms and stirring up even more anxieties for ourselves.

When you experience anxiety and tenseness, take time to think it through. Can you hear an old expectation from a parent or a teacher? Is that expectation realistic now? Is there a different message you long to hear? It is there. Read Psalm 139.

Saturday • One of the things, as sailors know, that can happen in a storm is that we can become consumed by the storm itself and forget how to navigate. As a result, a raging storm can swamp us and even take our lives. Our radar's gone out, and we feel there is no way to relieve the heavy weariness that settles around us.

We get so used to the feeling of fear or anxiety that we think there is no other way to be. We lose sight of the God who has promised to always be with us, to come to us in the storm, and be by our side...to be our radar.

But there is another way to consider storms. If Peter and the disciples had known the storm was coming, they would not have set out in the boat. They would have missed the storm, and they would have missed the encounter with Christ. Peter would not have had the opportunity to grow in his faith in Christ.

In our storms and anxieties, do we feel so frightened and alone that we do not recognize God there with us? In our storms and anxieties, do we recognize the opportunity to encounter Christ?

Week 31: From Anxiety to Peace

But when the disciples saw him walking on the lake, they were terrified, saying, "It is a ghost!" And they cried out in fear. But immediately Jesus spoke to them and said, "Take heart, it is I; do not be afraid." Peter answered him, "Lord, if it is you, command me to come to you on the water."–MATTHEW 14:26–28

Sunday • The disciples, according to Matthew's account, find themselves in the middle of an unexpected storm on the Sea of Galilee. They are understandably afraid, just as we often are when sudden storms invade our lives. In the midst of the surrounding chaos we hear Jesus say, as he said to his disciples, "Take heart, it is I; do not be afraid."

Those are the words Christ speaks to us when the winds and waves are about to sink our boat. These words—if we will but trust them—bring new strength, new courage, and new hope into our hearts. When we are torn apart by guilt and shame, Christ speaks to us and says, "Be of good cheer, your sins are forgiven; I remember them no more." When our hearts are overwhelmed by fear and worry and anxiety, Christ speaks to us and says, "Take heart; cast all your cares upon me for I care for you; you are in my everlasting arms." When we are at the breaking point, unsure that we can take one step more, Christ tells us his grace is all we need. Such is the way of our gracious Savior; always in the hour of our most desperate need, when strengths and hopes are nearly gone, when we are weary and beaten, he comes to us with his gracious words, "Take heart, it is I; do not be afraid." Can you (really) hear those words?

Monday • In the Gospel of Matthew, Jesus speaks to the frightened disciples. He says, "It is I; do not be afraid." He is speaking to us. He reminds us, as the beautiful hymn says, "Be Not

Afraid...I Go Before You Always." What a powerful, beautiful message. So what am I afraid of? What are you afraid of?

Of course, fear can motivate us. A bad cholesterol report can motivate us to eat a more healthy diet. A failing grade can motivate us to study harder. A threat of job loss or divorce can move us into recovery.

Jesus is talking about the fears that limit us, the fears that keep us from pushing ourselves toward important goals, the fears that restrain us from living life abundantly. The things we are afraid of mask the places we feel most vulnerable. Fear hides the places we are afraid to let others see or know about. I'm afraid to let anyone know how vulnerable and weak I am. Fear says, "Keep those places hidden at all cost!"

Where does fear limit your life? How would you finish this sentence, "If you really knew me..."? Does your answer reveal one of your fears? Christ knows you behind the mask and says, "Do not be afraid."

Tuesday • What would your life look like if you were not afraid—afraid of rejection, afraid of failing, afraid of making the wrong choice? Though axioms are often trite, they also contain some significant truths. "No decision is a decision" and "If nothing changes, nothing changes" are worth considering when we think about our fears.

Fear limits are lives, our choices, our opportunity to live life as God wants us to live it. One of the Church Fathers once said, "The glory of God is the human being fully alive." How dare we let fear rule our life! How dare we let fear motivate us to keep the mask between us and those we trust and love.

What mask are you wearing? Is there a secret you fear people might learn? Does that secret keep you isolated?

Wednesday • We all search for answers. Fear motivates us to watch ads, listen to advice columnists, read self-help books, and contact friends who have our best interests at heart. But we're not certain who or what to trust.

Christ speaks the words, "Do not be afraid." Do we even hear those words in the midst of our storms? Can we hear them when we're mired in our addiction or relapse? Are we so frightened that we don't hear Christ's words above the roar of the wind? If we begin to hear them, do we trust those words? Do we trust Christ when he says he is with us? When we feel so alone, how can we be sure he is there?

In this gospel reading, even Peter questions if Christ is there. He says, "Lord, if it is really you...." We know he is there because he has promised. Where do you hear the promise? Can you trust it?

Thursday • It can be so very difficult to trust a promise. All of us have had promises made to us by people we trusted, only to find the promises broken—by parents, siblings, spouses, bosses, and teachers. And all of us have broken promises we have made to other people. We relapse time and again, even after we have promised those we love that we will not drink or drug or watch porn or binge/purge or gamble or whatever the demon. When we break a promise, we feel guilty. We have broken a trust.

God promises us that he is with us always. He promises us that our sins are forgiven. He promises us he will save us from all our enemies—our dishonesty, our tempers, our addictions. And he will "bear us up as on eagle's wings." Forgiven. As a woman in Bible class once said, "That's just too good to be true." It does feel too good to be true. But trust in God's promises is called "faith." It can't be proved, but it can be felt as a presence in our lives.

What broken promises—yours or someone else's—leave you

with a sense of distrust? Do you believe you are forgiven—that God's promise is true?

Friday • What we seek in the middle of our personal storms is for the clouds to begin to break up, for a lightness to appear in the sky, and for the winds to settle down. We don't necessarily demand that the storm be over. In the sport of canoeing there is a level of participation called "still-water canoeing." Still waters are what we look for in the midst of our storms. Still waters promise rest and peace.

The peace we long for is already available in our lives. It is the gift of the Holy Spirit. When you are given a gift, what do you do? You thank the giver and you use the gift. You don't hide it in a drawer or place it on a shelf.

Where is the gift of peace in your life? Name it. How do you begin to recognize it, to use it?

Saturday • The gift of peace comes with strings attached. The strings are that we have to "follow the instructions" and "use as directed." Way too often when I am given a gift, I don't take the time to read the directions. I am excited, so I plug it in or put it on, thinking I know how to use it or that I'll figure it out as I go along. When it doesn't work correctly, I get frustrated and think the item must be broken. It couldn't be me! In recovery we attend meetings and follow the program...but only so far. We begin to think we really don't need to follow the directions we're given. All too often, we begin to slip back into our old ways.

God promises us peace, but we don't always know how to use it. We don't know how to put it on in the middle of a storm. It's as if we're drowning and have a life preserver in our hands, but we haven't belted it on. Or we don't trust it to keep us safe. God's gift of peace is available. It comes with instructions on how to use it in our daily lives: reading Scripture, partaking in

Eucharist, praying. It's a gift. And it's all ours if we just "belt it on."

Do you follow the Holy Spirit's "instructions" in your daily life?

Week 32: Come

Peter answered him, "Lord, if it is you, command me to come to you on the water." He said, "Come."–MATTHEW 14:28–29

Sunday • In the midst of this terrible storm on the Sea of Galilee, Christ appears to his friends by actually walking on the water. The bold disciple, their leader, Peter, says, "Lord, if it is you, command me to come to you on the water." Peter wasn't sure what he was seeing. "If" this is really you, he says. And Christ, always eager to respond to any request, says to Peter, "Come."

Come is such a gracious and inviting word. "Come to me, all you that are weary and carrying heavy burdens, and I will give you rest" (Matthew 11:28). Come to me with your lives—lives that are so often narrow and cramped with limited horizons and selfish self-interests. Come to me with your lives that are crowded with trifles and insignificant ambitions. Come to me even when you feel you are without direction and purpose. Come, enter the full, rich, and abundant life I offer you. Walk with me in the way of discipleship. Come and join me in my mission to save the broken world. With that simple invitation—come—he holds before us a vision of what life might be: a glorious and grand adventure without equal. He is waiting for our response.

Monday • Through this devotion we are encouraged to think about our lives—not just the storms and anxieties, but our lives as a whole. The storms and anxieties distract us and keep us limited. They keep us "in the boat." Our daily lives can absorb all our time and energy. The "busyness" of work, family, and pleasure fills up our days. And at the end of a nonstop day, we pause to wonder, *What did I accomplish today? What am I accomplishing with my life?*

Both my eighteen-year-old grandson and an eighty-year-old friend recently asked out loud, "Who am I?" We become self-absorbed with school or work and neglect to reflect on our bigger life. Who are we, really?

What is your bigger life? What were the dreams you had as a young person? Where is your spiritual life in all of this? Are you accomplishing what you want in your relationship with God?

Tuesday • The disciples were terrified when they first saw Jesus walking on the water. They screamed, and Jesus spoke to them at once. We all have fear-filled moments. Maybe we don't scream out loud, but we know how fear can immobilize us. I remember once seeing a man looking in my bedroom window, and I was so terrified, I couldn't move, nor could I scream.

In our most terrified times as well as in our daily lives, Jesus will speak to us at once...if we will only ask and listen. He always wants connection with us. He says, "Have courage... it is I." We can hear those words when we follow up on that doctor's appointment even when we fear the news. He says, "Have courage!" when we set limits on our daughter's behavior, even when we fear she will be angry with us. He says, "Have courage!" when we admit we were wrong in an argument with our spouse. He says, "Have courage!" when we make that first phone call to our sponsor.

At the close of your day, think of the times you had courage this day. You did the right thing. You chose the way of discipleship. Were you aware of Christ with you? Did you realize it was Christ who gave you that courage?

Wednesday • When we hear Christ say, "Come," as he did to Peter, we often don't know exactly what that means. Try to remember some of your earlier dreams and ambitions. Maybe you wanted to make a real contribution to the world. You felt you could make "a difference." But then someone may have said, "You're not smart enough" or "You can't afford that training" or "You have other things you have to do." But those dreams may have been Christ's way of saying, "Come!" Somehow, between those dreams, you have made this your life with all the good and the bad "stuff" that has occurred. And through it all, Christ never stops saying, "Come to me."

Today is a new day. We can "Come," come and follow Christ into a life of discipleship. Simply put, discipleship means responding to Christ's call of obedience...obedience within this new life he offers us. Obedience to his call to "Love one another."

Where today can you move into this life of discipleship? Is it about a gentle word to a coworker who really irritates you? Is it about phoning an older friend who may be lonely? Is it about choosing not to go to the bar even for a soft drink? Does it feel like a new life, a life of discipleship?

Thursday • Peter asks Christ to bid him come to him on the water. Peter stopped being afraid long enough to ask for a connection with Christ. He wasn't certain the figure on the water was Christ, but he longed for that connection enough to risk getting out of his comfort zone. Our usual comfort zone defines who we are, what risks we are willing to take, where our lives remain. When we risk getting out of our boat—out of our comfort zone—we have an opportunity to encounter our lives and our relationship with Christ in a new way. When we begin to frame our thinking in discipleship, we begin to frame our thoughts, our behaviors, and our decisions in the framework of "What is the loving thing to do here?" That can be a risk.

And it might take us out of our comfort zone. But it's worth it!

Christ bids us to "Come"—risk a new life, a spiritual deepening, a new encounter with him.

What new behavior or decision would move you in spiritual deepening? How might that spiritual deepening be evident to those around you?

Friday • The word *discipleship* has a very serious ring to it. Thinking of ourselves as disciples sounds like an ominous undertaking, and we may not feel up to it. Yet Christ calls us to that very thing and assures us that he came so that we might have life and have it abundantly. What on earth does *abundantly* mean? That really doesn't sound like the seriousness of discipleship.

Abundantly means a richness to life, an overflowing fullness, a great plenty. That is the life Christ wants us to have in discipleship. He wants our discipleship to feel like fun and adventure and fullness. When we live abundantly, we experience a richness of connection with those we love and with Christ.

Is there a sense of great plenty in your life? Where? When? Often in new recovery, there is that "pink cloud" of great plenty. How do you make that last?

Saturday• When we want to experience more of that abundant sense of overflowing fullness, we may have to take some risks. We might have to stretch beyond our comfort zone. That feeling of fullness can come in many ways. Combining your early dreams with a deeper search for spirituality can lead to the sense of fulfillment and connection. Taking time to talk honestly with a trusted friend when you feel alone and afraid builds a connection, an intimacy. Joining someone in a raucous belly laugh reminds us that Christ wants us to be joyful. We are created to laugh and he wants to be there, enjoying it all with us. He is waiting for our response.

What is your response? Where in your life might you "come" to Christ as a deeply connected disciple?

Week 33: Out of the Boat

He said, "Come." So Peter got out of the boat, started walking on the water, and came toward Jesus. But when he noticed the strong wind, he became frightened, and beginning to sink, he cried out, "Lord, save me!" Jesus immediately reached out his hand and caught him. –MATTHEW 14:29–31

Sunday • When Jesus invites Peter to leave the boat and walk on the water to him, Peter does exactly that. But then (how like Peter—indeed, how like us) he takes his eyes off Christ and sees only the waves. He is terrified.

Peter was bold. Peter was strong, but when he took his eyes off Christ and focused on the wind and the waves, he started to sink. He forgot that Christ was there. He concentrated only on the dark and the deep, and he started to go under.

Isn't this also our story? Instead of fixing our attention on Christ and trusting his presence-promises, in the time of impossible stress and struggle, we look only at our troubles and problems, and it overwhelms us. We begin to sink!

If only we would look to Christ at such times, fix our gaze on him, we'd experience how Peter felt when that strong arm caught him. We'd be flooded with a sense of peace, knowing nothing—absolutely nothing—can separate us from his love. It is that promise that steadies us and keeps us afloat.

Monday • As we read this devotion, we remember that Peter wasn't certain the form he was seeing was really Christ. *Should I do this? Does he want me to come to him? Ask me to come to you, Christ!* Then he heard Christ's voice, "Come."

Often our addictions, our attachments, our priorities, prompt us to say, "I don't want to listen. I don't even want to see him. I have other priorities now." If I heard him say "Come," it might make me change my life. I don't want to invite him into my life right now. "Don't ask me to come to you, Christ." Or we may have attended church in our youth, but as we grew up, we became busy with our friends, distracted. We took our eyes off Christ.

In our times of struggle and even in our quiet, daily lives, do we ask Christ to bid us to come? Or do we just hope Christ will come into our lives? Do we just hope we will see an image, feel a presence that will assure us he is there?

Tuesday • What happens if we do hear Christ's call to "Come"? Is that call too faint to hear? We hear other voices, other calls, much more loudly, and it's those calls that get our attention. We hear the call of money, the call of a career, the call of a drug.

Furthermore, we're far too busy to listen. We tell ourselves we are way too busy...way too busy to call that elderly person; she will want to talk forever. We're way too busy to go to church; we have to do all the laundry on Saturday, and Johnny has a soccer game Sunday morning. We're way too busy to pray, "Command me to come."

Do daily struggles and storms cause you to miss the call to "Come"?

Wednesday • It is not unusual in a time of crisis to hear a person exclaim, "Oh, my God!" Unfortunately, more often than not, this exclamation is not a prayer or cry for help. It's simply a manner of expressing surprise or concern. We use it in short-hand texting. It seems our culture has come to the point that we shorthand and shortchange what should be an intentional message to God...a message of "command me to come."

Where in your life do you ask Christ, "Command me to come"? How would that look in your day?

Thursday • Jesus said words of encouragement in his call to Peter. "Take heart…do not be afraid" (Matthew 14:27). But where do we find the courage to make the changes that will lead us into this wonderful world of adventure and growth with Christ, this discipleship?

When we are consumed by health problems, when we fear for a child in trouble, when a relapse in our own addictions is across the table, how do we keep our gaze on Christ? How do we get out of our boat, out of our little routines that keep us so busy and so distant from a relationship with Christ? Where do we find the courage to make Christ our priority and to keep our gaze firmly fixed?

We find the courage in his promises of peace. He said, "My peace I give to you" (John 14:27). He promises us peace when we hear "It is I" in daily prayer, "This is my Body" in the Eucharist.

What attachments or priorities distract you today? What small change can you make in your day to keep your eyes fixed on Christ? Before you go to sleep, ask yourself, "Where did I see Christ today?"

Friday • When we feel ourselves sinking and overcome by fear, we can pray as Peter did, "Lord, save me!" And at once Jesus reaches out his hand and grabs hold of us. When fear leaves us, our whole body responds in a healthy, healing way. Like a loving parent, Jesus cradles us in his arms. We might not always recognize that cradling, but when we take the time to notice that we're not really sinking, we feel his loving embrace.

When the storm has passed, our feelings of loneliness may still come and go. But as Christians, we have an insurance policy, an annuity, with promises and benefits. Christ promises to be with us. It is up to us as disciples to study those benefits and to collect on those promises.

All disciples, as Peter did, continue to grow in faith. We grow spiritually by reminding ourselves to be awake, to recognize Christ in storms and in the calm. Without paying attention to his promises, we will not recognize him and we may miss his presence with us, his peace.

What are Christ's promises? How are they relevant in your daily life?

Saturday • This new strength that gives us the courage to get out of our boat, to ask Christ to bid us come, to respond to his call to "Come," is the Holy Spirit dwelling within us.

When we're in the midst of a storm, it's sometimes hard to recognize the Spirit within us. But we can recognize it in others. One day I watched my son, an active-duty Marine, interact with a severely disabled child in the most gentle, delightful manner. They laughed, they joked, and they played for a very long time. This son of mine, to my knowledge, had not been around a person with disabilities for any length of time. But he entered this new water with ease and trusted that it would be safe. It was a spiritual moment reflective of another gift of the Holy Spirit—the gift of gentleness. Christ said, "Come," and Jack responded. While it wasn't an earth-shattering moment, the joy around his actions changed the day for all of us.

Are you aware of the Spirit alive within you, Christ bidding you to "Come"? When are you aware of it? How do you respond?

Week 34: Saving Hands

Jesus immediately reached out his hand and caught him.

–MATTHEW 14:31

Sunday • When a storm on the Sea of Galilee caught the disciples by surprise, they were scared to death. In spite of the crashing waves, they could see Jesus coming toward them. Peter was so excited that, without thinking, he jumped into the water. But then he realized what he'd done and began to sink. Then Jesus does a wonderful thing: He reaches out his hand to Peter and saves him!

Often we think that saints are people who never fail. We think they have everything together and never embarrass themselves, that they have no weaknesses or shortcomings. But that's a misconception. Rather, a saint is a disciple who jumps in, gets wet, begins to sink, but relies on Christ to help him or her get back up. It's not the sinking or the falling that is the worst but the staying down. We may trip over our weaknesses and stumble over our shortcomings, but Christ is always there, reaching out his hands to pull us back up and set us on our way.

And we recognize those hands. They still bear the prints of the nails that fastened him to the cross where he gave his life for us so that we can be his people.

Monday • When we are struggling in a storm or just trying to get by each day, it's difficult to see the hand that is extended to us. We are proud, we are stubborn, we are selfish. If we need a "hand up," we fear the other person will think we are weak, inadequate, less than perfect. Whenever I find myself in a new job, I think, "Well, here I am. They have to think I can do this all by myself." That's me, trying to be "all competent" again.

Before I entered recovery, I struggled about how much I might drink on a given day. I always thought I could handle it.

I couldn't ask my husband or a friend to help me with this because then they might know. They might know I'm not perfect.

The stress and pain we put ourselves through because we can't see the hand that is reaching out to us!

Who in your life is reaching out to you? Are you able to stretch your hand for help?

Tuesday • As Peter took his eyes off Christ and felt himself sinking, he cried out, "Save me, Lord!" It's a desperate cry. It's the cry we make when we pace the floor at two AM, fearful that we are sinking—sinking from our own misplaced priorities, our own poor decisions, our own demons. It's the cry of, "Good God, what am I going to do about this?" We are crying for help, but we don't even know to whom we are crying. It's the "OMG!" that feels like crying into cyberspace.

But like Peter, if we squint through the wind and the rain, we begin to recognize who is there, holding out his hand toward us. When we recognize him, we can stop flailing and drowning. We can experience an overwhelming sense of peace. That person may not look like Christ, but Christ comes to us in surprising ways.

We may actually pray, "Save me, Lord!" In that moment, we feel his strength—and his peace.

Can you utter the cry? "Save me, Lord! Save me from the storm and save me in my everyday. Save all whom I love. Bring them calm and peace in their storms."

Wednesday • Whom do you think of as a saint? Is it Saint Joseph, kind and patient with the child Jesus? Is it Saint Teresa, full of goodness and humility? We recognize wonderful, beautiful saints whose lives are examples of faithfulness. But what about Saint Peter? Here was a saint who took his eyes off Christ and began to sink. He denied Christ three times the night before the crucifixion. He knew what it was like to fail.

We are all Peters; we're saints who fail. We constantly slip into our old patterns of anger, resentment, gossip, lying, and misplaced priorities such as money, career, and possessions. We take our eyes off Christ. We neglect to ask him to save us. And we ignore the hand he extends to us.

What are you most at risk of "slipping" in to? What prevents you from knowing at a very deep level that Christ is with you—always?

Thursday • No one wants to be a loser. No one deliberately chooses to fail. But addiction is a fatal disease. That's the tragedy of the "slip" or relapse for the alcoholic or drug addict. We might well die if the addiction consumes us. When the priority that consumes us, that causes us to take our eyes off Christ, is more of an attachment, we may not see a slip or relapse as quite as fatal. But the anxiety and the loneliness and the emptiness of those pursuits can be fatal to our soul, to our sense of connection and relationship with Christ.

When we realize we have failed, that we have fallen, the tragedy is not in the fall but in the reluctance to get up. The urge to just stay down, to give up, can be so appealing. After all, we have tried to overcome those bad habits, bad choices, and old patterns of poor decisions over and over.

But have our attempts been another pattern of self-absorption: "I can do this by myself…I don't need anyone, especially not God!" Have we neglected to ask God to save us?

What feels like failure in your life? What feels like success? Where do you recognize Christ most?

Friday • Storms occur in our lives that have nothing to do with our poor choices, bad decisions, or bad habits. Some storms just descend on us. We are unable to avoid them. They are simply circumstances that occur in life—sometimes very tragic occurrences, sometimes just the little stuff that keeps happening over and over again.

Then there are times that life seems to be going OK. We can't see any gathering clouds on the horizon. We feel safe.

Whatever our circumstance, Christ's hands reach out to us; he is always there.

How have you sensed his presence, in the good times and in the bad?

Saturday • The hands that reach out to us we sometimes recognize as Christ's because we see the nail scars. He gave his life so we might live and live life abundantly. Other hands may not be so readily identified. But Christ is there in all those hands that remind us we no longer need a life of fear, of loneliness. He wants us to know ourselves as forgiven, blessed, and beloved. He wants us to know ourselves as his children. He will always have his hands held out to us. We only need to keep our eyes fixed on him and call out, "Save me!" He is there with us. That is his promise.

Do we have the faith to believe in that promise? Can we reach out? Do we trust?

Week 35: Into the Deep

He got into one of the boats, the one belonging to Simon, and asked him to put out a little way from the shore. Then he sat down and taught the crowds from the boat. When He had finished speaking, he said to Simon, 'Put out into the deep water and let down your nets for a catch. Simon answered, 'Master, we have worked all night long but have caught nothing. Yet if you say so, I will let down the nets.' When they had done this, they caught so many fish that their nets were beginning to break.

—LUKE 5:3–6

Sunday • This encounter of Jesus with Peter and his fishermen friends shows Jesus involved in our daily lives. Peter and his friends were frustrated because they weren't catching anything. Jesus saw this and said, "Put out into the deep water and let down your nets for a catch." When they did this, they brought up such a large catch of fish that their nets began to break. That miracle wonderfully transformed their lives. They left their boats and followed him.

That is what happens when Christ encounters us. He reworks our lives with his grace and accomplishes a miracle in our lives. He encounters us with his overwhelming love and changes our hearts. We become new people with a new way of living.

Notice in this encounter with Peter that it was Jesus who made the first move. He initiated it. He came to Peter and his friends. And so it is with us. Christ makes the first move; he initiates the encounter. And look at how he often does it. He comes to us in our hopelessness, our worries and anxieties, our despair, our pain, our struggles, our "fishing all night and catching nothing," and uses those experiences to turn our lives around and to encounter us—to offer us a new life with hope and joy and healing and purpose. That's the amazing grace of Jesus Christ.

Monday • Do you fish? How frustrating that sport can be! We stand on the shore or in the boat casting our lines, and nothing happens. The bobber teases us with nibbles. Maybe we get a bite, but when we reel it in, the bait is gone and we have no fish. Down the shoreline or out in another boat, in a different spot, we see other fishermen hauling in nice catches.

That is so like life. We work and work, seemingly getting nowhere. We become frustrated with our lives and our efforts. We look for a different spot, and nothing changes; still no big catch. We feel like we are trying hard, that something ought to work—until the still, small voice within us begins to speak a new message.

Jesus spoke to the disciples, "Put out into the deep and let down your nets…"

Do you sometimes hear a "still, small voice" that speaks about risk and change, that says, "Put out into the deep"?

Tuesday • When the "still, small voice" begins to give us direction and lead us in a new way, do we listen? Or do we say, like Peter might have, "Oh, come on. I've fished all night and nothing happens." In our heads we might say, "Oh, I've tried to stop drinking or smoking or spending, but nothing ever changes." We become so frustrated and disappointed by our efforts that we lose courage to try something new.

But if we listen to this voice, we hear a loving command, a direction, "Put out into the deep water and let down your nets." Now there's something exciting—"put out into the deep." Christ is not telling us to stay safely on the shore. He's saying "go out to the deep"—try something really new! Have courage!

What would "putting out into the deep" mean for you? How might your life change if you stepped "out into the deep"?

Wednesday • We come back to the issue of trust. Do we trust God in the risen Christ? Do we trust we are safe in his promise? When we think about "putting out into the deep water," we are talking about risks that lead us to a closer relationship with God. We might have to give up something. When we struggle with an attachment or addiction that is truly destructive, we long to trust "putting out into the deep and letting down our nets" once again, even though we may have "fished all night." Peter said, "I'll do it if you say so." We hear the same voice Peter heard, telling us of the possibility of a miracle in our lives.

In addition to the very destructive behaviors we might be trapped in, we can also experience small changes that transform our lives. We can be with other people in ways that reflect God's mercy and grace in our lives. It may be as simple as a loving word to our children and our spouse as they leave for the morning. Or it may be an offer of help to a coworker who is stressed or hugging a sick friend.

Do you trust that God is with you "in the deep"? How does that make you feel?

Thursday • Peter and his friends were cleaning their nets, doing their work just as they did most nights. Jesus came to them. They weren't in the synagogue on their knees; they were doing their job. Christ comes to us in our everyday struggles too. It's just that so very often we overlook the fact that he is there. We miss the evidence of his grace in our lives. We miss an openness and awareness of his presence. But he continues to come to us over and over again. That is God's amazing grace.

We can be certain because God says so. Each time God comes to us, he is offering us his love, his forgiveness, and a new life. We just have to pay attention.

Are you paying attention to Christ's encounters with you each day? How do you know that? Where? When?

Friday • We pay attention to Christ's presence when we attend church and every other day when we pray and when we reflect his love to others. My friend works for a company that recently lost a large, lucrative contract. The loss of that contract could cost many jobs. My friend manages this division, and she cried as the shock of the loss became clear to her. Her response was, "Of course I care about the contract, but the real tragedy is for Melinda and the others whose jobs are at risk. Melinda is a single woman, alone, and undergoing radiation for cancer. What will she do? How can I be there for her?"

Without really realizing it, this supervisor was asking herself, "How can I go into the deep for her?" Soon she was able to think of ways she could protect Melinda, find a new space for her in another contract. Her care and concern for her coworker reflect Christ's love and protection for all of us.

Do you go into the deep for others in a way that reflects Christ's love?

Saturday • Peter's nets were empty, but in our culture of consumerism, we sometimes miss the fact that our nets are so very full. We have plenty, yet we buy into the advertising and want more and more, bigger and bigger, newer and newer. So we work harder and longer hours, hoping to "fill our nets," to fill the void. We miss the point that the "catch" Christ promises us is a closer relationship with him. He urges us to take risks, to go into the deep, to cast our nets—to get rid of the anxieties and attachments and addictions that keep us from this new life of hope and joy and healing. He urges us to have courage and trust that our lives have purpose.

Does your life have purpose and meaning? What happens when you go beyond thinking about goals and consider the ultimate purpose of your life?

Week 36: Sinful Man

When they had done this, they caught so many fish that their nets were beginning to break. So they signaled their partners in the other boat to come and help them. And they came and filled both boats, so that they began to sink. But when Simon Peter saw it, he fell down at Jesus' knees, saying, "Go away from me, Lord, for I am a sinful man!"—LUKE 5:6–9

Sunday • Peter is the recipient of a miracle while fishing on the Sea of Galilee. He has fished all night and has caught nothing; that is, until Christ comes along and tells him to cast his nets into the deep. The result is that the nets are filled with fish.

And how would you expect Peter to respond? We would think Peter would be overjoyed at his good fortune, but instead, he acknowledges his unworthiness. He says, "Go away from me, Lord, for I am a sinful man!"

Why this response? Because Peter operates with the notion that many of us hold, which is that good people are rewarded and bad people are punished. Peter knows himself to be a sinner—one who has no regard for the law or for religion and therefore one who deserves to be punished. But Christ reverses that notion. He floods the life of Peter with his love. That's what causes Peter to confess his unworthiness.

And that's God's way with us. We may have given up on ourselves, believing that we have so often disgraced God by our behavior that there is no hope for us. But this miraculous catch of fish tells us that God never gives up on us, that his mercy is greater than our sin and that his love is greater than our unfaithfulness. Just when we think we are going to come under the heavy hand of God's punishment, he lavishes his forgiving grace on us. What a reversal! Thank God!

Monday • Though he has fished all night, Peter follows Christ's direction and lowers his nets once again. A miracle occurs. His nets are filled to overflowing. Has a miracle ever occurred in your life? Have you called what happened a miracle? Did you laugh? Cry?

If the miracle in our lives happens spontaneously, we are usually overjoyed. Depending on our personalities, we might jump and shout, or we might quietly share the news with friends and neighbors. But either way, we'd likely think, "What luck!"

Miracles can be slow in occurring and hard to recognize when they happen. After all, we may have cast our nets for years and years trying to catch this miracle. But when we recognize the miracle as real, we often take most of the credit ourselves. We may say, "Well, I finally did it. I changed the way I was doing things" or "I changed my attitude" or "If I didn't stop, I was going to die."

We often miss the fact that the miracle occurred because we followed Christ's direction. We listened to the still, small voice that called to us.

What miracle in your life might you have missed naming? What miracle occurred that you took credit for? What was Christ's direction that you followed?

Tuesday • As the Sunday meditation tells us, Peter had an unusual response to the miracle of the catch of fish. He said, "Go away from me, Lord, for I am a sinful man!" Peter's response acknowledges that he had absolutely nothing to do with the miracle. It was simply God's good and gracious love that provided this miracle. Peter felt he shouldn't even be in the company of Christ. Peter felt his sin made him unworthy to receive this miracle or to be in the presence of Christ.

When a miracle occurs in our lives, at the center of our being, we may also feel unworthy. We know ourselves to be sinners.

We've distanced ourselves from God by making other things the priorities in our lives. And then all of a sudden, or sometimes more slowly, we recognize the miracle. God's love has helped us recognize his presence in our lives. This miracle reminds us that he is always with us, no matter what our sin.

Do you recognize the miracle of healing that happens each day in your life?

Wednesday • The miracles we look for are often related to physical healing for ourselves or those we love. But often the healing we need most is the healing of our souls. Like Peter, we know we have sinned. We have caused other people pain and anguish. We have made our attachments, our resentments, and our addictions the priorities in our lives. We have not given of our time or talents to others who need us. We feel this conflict as stress in our bodies and emptiness in our souls—the God-shaped void. We know we are "unworthy."

And then God provides a miracle to remind us that he is always there. He never gives up on us. When we are reminded of Christ's presence, we may rejoice or we may quietly say "thank you," but most important, we recognize that it is a sign of Christ's overflowing love.

In the Catholic liturgy at Eucharist, we pray, "Lord, I am not worthy that you should enter under my roof, but only say the word and my soul shall be healed." Remember this beautiful prayer as you approach the altar.

How do you respond to the daily miracles in your life? Do you think about them at the close of each day?

Thursday• In our self-centered, self-promoting society, humility is not popular. It's not cool to say we're not worthy. That implies being a loser. Generally we hear athletes, businesspeople, entertainment stars, even people who win the lottery brashly attribute this glory to their success, to their hard work, or to luck. Rarely do they call it a miracle. Rarely do they glimpse God working in their lives.

It is difficult to look inside ourselves and honestly say, "I am not worthy. This miracle of my life is a gift from God. All of this is a sign that God never gives up on me."

What causes you to feel unworthy of God's great love? How does it feel to acknowledge that unworthiness and yet begin to accept his love as real and present in your life?

Friday • Once we begin to accept the reality of God's love and presence in our lives, we experience an incredible sense of peace. The daily miracles become frequent signs of his desire to show us he is here.

As I write this, I look out my window and see the sun rising on the drops of frost on the ground. The drops are sparkling, and I am reminded of the love song that refers to diamonds and the morning dew. It is God's love that gives me diamonds on the morning dew—day after day. I am not worthy of diamonds, but still God gives them to me.

Have you sensed the miracle of God's presence in your life today?

Saturday • This conflict between feeling unworthy to be in God's presence and yet recognizing God's forgiving grace and love in our lives is a miraculous new way of living. Yes, we are unworthy. No, there is no way we merit or earn God's love. But to recognize ourselves as deeply cherished and forgiven provides us with such hope. When we have God's promise of forgiveness, we can follow his direction to push into the deep, cast our nets, and know the miracle of his love in our lives.

What new direction does God's love and forgiveness give to your life?

Week 37: Do Not Be Afraid

Then Jesus said to Simon, "Do not be afraid; from now on you will be catching people."...They left everything and followed him.

—LUKE 5:10–11

Sunday • Peter's encounter with the unexpected grace of God at the miraculous catch of fish causes him to say, "Go away from me, for I am a sinful man!"

But Christ does not leave Peter alone. And he doesn't abandon us either. Instead, he accepts us unconditionally. That means there are no conditions. He doesn't say, "I will accept you if you shape up" or "I will accept you if you clean up your act" or "I will accept you if you once and for all give up your addictions and attachments." No. He accepts us as we are; he is not ashamed to be called our brother.

And what's more astonishing is that he actualizes his forgiveness. He calls us to follow him. He wants us to be his disciples, his partners. Like Peter, we're tempted to say, "Go away from me, for I am sinful," and Christ says, "Do not be afraid"; join me...join me in my great work of healing this broken world. Join me in bringing my love to those who daily struggle with depression and despair. Join me in bringing my mercy to those who have fallen and cannot get up again.

Monday • Peter was astounded and shocked at the miracle of Christ's filling his nets with fish, filling them to overflowing. He recognized the divinity of Christ.

We see many examples of times and moments of people beginning to have a sense of faith. I am reminded of a book by C.S. Lewis entitled *Surprised by Joy*. When I first heard that title, I assumed it was a book about his beloved wife, whose name was Joy. But the book concerns the movement of the agnostic Lewis to the person-of-belief Lewis. The book recalls the joy Lewis felt as he came to an understanding of God's gift of grace and forgiveness. This was a brilliant man who taught at Oxford University, wrote extensively, and before his conversion argued emphatically with his colleagues about the existence of God. After his movement to Christ, he "pushed into the deep" and wrote the Narnia books, all of which can be interpreted as books of deep faith.

The brothers of Vermont's Weston Priory sing of "the morning I knew you came into my life." It's a hymn of faith, and these miracle lyrics are ours.

Was there a moment you knew Christ came into your life, or was it more of an ever-increasing awareness, some quiet time of being touched? With that awareness, is there a joy, a relief, a peace?

Tuesday • Even though Peter tells Christ to "go away" from him, Christ does not leave. Peter has difficulty accepting that Christ really and truly is in his life. We, too, have difficulty accepting that Christ is in our lives. We have difficulty believing that even when we tell him to "go away," he stays around. He is there no matter how long we have ignored him. He stays no matter how many ways we have offended him and sinned against him.

In our human frailty, we put conditions on our love even with those we care most about, so it's very hard to understand and accept that God puts no conditions on his love for us. The great news is that we don't have to understand it! We only have to begin to believe that he does. And even that is hard. As mentioned before, when we talk about unconditional love in our Bible class, one woman says with a somewhat disbelieving smile, "That's just too good to be true." That's where the term *good news* comes from. It is Good News!

Do you believe God puts conditions on his love for you? Can

you begin to let go of that? Can you begin to accept that the Good News really is good news for you?

Wednesday • God tells us in so many ways that he accepts us as we are. He tells us he is our Father. He calls us his children. He gives us his Son, and that makes Christ our brother. We are members of his family; we are in relationship with him.

If we truly are a part of God's family, if Christ is our "brother," what does this mean? If we have brothers or sisters, we often fuss with them, but we also know that no one else better criticize them. We will stick up for them against any others. The military uses the term *band of brothers*. By that, they mean they will defend one another and fight for one another even unto death.

God gave us his Son to help us fight our enemies daily. God gave us his Son to fight for us even unto death.

When you take time to consider Christ as your brother, what does it say about God's love for you?

Thursday • In this Scripture from the Gospel of Luke, Christ responds to Peter's declaration of sinfulness by saying, "Do not be afraid; from now on you will be catching people." If only we could really believe that we don't need to be afraid of Christ's response to our sin. Of course, our sin has consequences in our everyday lives and with Christ. These consequences can be serious and require our confession, repentance, and apology to those we have offended. We confess to friends and family and we confess to God.

Often it feels like the consequences never disappear in our daily lives. The people we have hurt carry that hurt and remind us of our shame. But Christ doesn't do that. He wants us to acknowledge our sins as did Peter, and then he says, "Do not be afraid; from now on you will be catching people."

Are you sometimes afraid of God's punishment for your

sins? Does Christ's reminder of "Do not be afraid" give some peace to your soul? How do you bring that peace of forgiveness into your daily life?

Friday • When Peter's nets were full to overflowing and it felt like the nets were breaking, they signaled their fishing partners in a nearby boat, and both nets were filled to overflowing. Scripture reminds us that Peter had partners. Christ does not expect us to join him in this "catching of people" by ourselves. When we have "pushed into the deep and let down our nets," we have partners with us as our nets fill to overflowing.

When Karen started her involvement with flood victims in her area, she really had no idea the amount of need or what her involvement would mean. She simply pushed into the deep. But as the awareness of the need increased, more and more "partners" joined her efforts. Many of her partners were from her parish and diocese. But many others came from other friends and members of the communities affected by the tropical storm's devastation. They practiced discipleship together.

Push into the deep...cast your nets...signal to partners... don't be afraid.

Who are your partners in following Christ?

Saturday • Peter and his partners "left everything and followed him." How could they do that? How could they give up their homes, their belongings, and leave their families? Leaving everything behind is not what our culture teaches us. Instead, we're told to collect more and more and more.

One way to consider "leaving everything" is to consider the words just before that: "Do not be afraid." Christ tells us to leave our fears—leave the fears that people will sneer at us if we reflect Christ in our daily lives; leave the fears that you won't be "up" to the task; leave the fears that if we reach out to our community with a community lunch or with a new Bible class or a new fundraiser, we won't be successful.

Christ simply asks that we follow him without fear.

If you had no fears, what adventure would you embark on to reflect Christ in your life?

The Power of Prayer

Sunday's focus is on prayer and what it might mean in our lives. Following this we will focus on the seven petitions of the Lord's Prayer.

Week 38: The Lord's Prayer

Our Father, who art in heaven,
hallowed be thy name;
thy kingdom come,
thy will be done
on earth as it is in heaven.
Give us this day our daily bread,
and forgive us our trespasses,
as we forgive those who trespass against us;
and lead us not into temptation,
but deliver us from evil. –MATTHEW 6:9–12

Sunday • Prayer is a wonderful gift that God has given us. When God invites us to pray, it's as if we can lay out our whole life and heart before him. We don't need to keep any secrets. God, in Christ, accepts us just as we are. Absolutely nothing in our lives is so insignificant that we need to keep it to ourselves any longer. God wants to hear about every aspect of our lives, big or small.

Just to have someone who is that interested in us is reason alone to pray. But there is another reason. Prayer is a necessary part of our relationship with God. If you had a close friend but never bothered to talk with him or her, what do you suppose would happen in that relationship? It would eventually shrivel and die. God wants to talk with us; he wants us to converse with him. Prayer is one of the great gifts God gives us by which he sustains his relationship with us.

Monday • Our reluctance to pray may come from many different parts of our lives. It may come from fear, fear of being judged, for instance. Our attachments, addictions, and priorities may have created pockets of embarrassment and shame. We may not want anyone to know we are in this deep place of anxiety or darkness. Turning to God in prayer seems like revealing our vulnerability. If we have grown up afraid of God, if we have been taught that God is full of judgment and anger, we are reluctant, even scared, to consider revealing this secret anxiety to him.

If we find ourselves in dark places that may not be of our own creation—illness, death, job loss—we might feel abandoned and reluctant to pray. We may even wonder, *What good is prayer? I haven't prayed for years. Why should God listen to me now?*

What is your current prayer life? Do you feel close to God when you pray?

Tuesday • Our reluctance to pray can also come from a sense of unworthiness. When we are depressed or have a poor image of ourselves, it is difficult to feel worthy of anyone's help—especially God's. We feel disconnected. We may feel we don't want to bother or upset anyone. When my daughter was killed in a traffic accident, I held in my grief around my family. They were suffering also, of course; nevertheless, I didn't want to upset them with my grief. I also didn't know what to pray. She was dead. Why pray? Why bother God at this point?

When people in recovery relapse time after time, they may feel unworthy and beyond help. They may also feel that their anxiety or concern is insignificant compared to someone else's emotional and mental state and that they are selfish to ask God for help.

But the reality is that God wants to be involved in our lives. If you are a parent, you know how wonderful it is when a child comes to you with his or her problems. We feel honored and close to them when they confide in us.

"Our Father…" Do you turn in prayer to God as a loving Father who feels honored when you turn to him?

Wednesday • Our prayer life with God is an essential part of our relationship with him. Prayer is asking and then giving God permission to help us. Even though we may feel embarrassed at our circumstances, unworthy of asking for help, or feel a problem is insignificant, when we pray we acknowledge to God and to ourselves that the relationship is intact and that we trust God's involvement in our lives.

A friend talks of his struggle to quit smoking. This is a very spiritual man who prays, "OK, God, I could use a little help here." There is no perfect way to pray. It is an ongoing conversation with the One who desires a relationship with us.

Do you give God permission to be involved in your life? How? When?

Thursday • If prayer is communication with God, we need to remember that communication is a two-way street. When we pray, we frequently ask for something, we do all the talking. What if we were quiet and just listened?

In all communication, whether spiritual or in our everyday relationships, it is helpful to remember that the emphasis needs to be on listening. With our spouse or at work, too often our priority is getting our needs met, asking for what we want, when in fact, the best relationships are built when we focus on what the other person has to say, what their needs are. God is beyond needing anything from us, but from what we read in the Bible, God relishes our relationship. All we need do is simply ask God to be present. And when we listen, we may not get an explanation of what is occurring in our lives, but God's guidance will become clearer.

When have you listened in prayer? Do you hear any of God's promises?

Friday • What if you haven't prayed for a long time? What if you are reluctant to start praying again? What if you are afraid that God has forgotten you, crossed you off his list? God in Christ is the most passionate friend we have ever had. He will never cross us off his list. He promises to be with us forever.

I move around a lot and am a pretty good correspondent with friends from previous locales. However sometimes I lose track of people. Maybe they move, maybe they change their e-mail address. Good friends, however, tend to reconnect. When that happens we hear the joy in their voices. "It's as if we've not been apart. We can pick up right where we left off!" Trusting and intimate relationships are like that.

That is what it is like when we start praying again. Christ is so delighted to hear from us.

Is it time to reconnect with Christ? Can we just talk and talk and talk? And then listen?

Saturday • Prayer is another one of God's exquisite gifts. Why wouldn't we use it? Prayer-gifts may come with directions such as in a book on how to meditate. Or a prayer-gift may come from a visit to church or a conversation with a friend. The important thing, if we are just getting back to prayer, is to "just do it." Begin to talk with God. Let him know what's going on in your life. Of course God already knows it all, the good stuff and the bad, but like a wonderful parent, he loves to hear it from you—again and again.

God, can we just be in touch?

Week 39: Our Father

And whenever you pray...pray then in this way:
"Our Father..."–MATTHEW 6:5, 9

Sunday • When the disciples ask Jesus to teach them to pray, he responds by saying, "Whenever you pray...." Notice that he doesn't say *if* you pray. Rather, it's *when* you pray, indicating that prayer is an important part of our relationship with him.

If we are honest, we would have to admit that often prayer is not a regular part of our lives. Why is that? Why do we have so much trouble with our prayer life instead of finding in it the real joy and substance of our existence? Why do we have to force ourselves to keep company with the heavenly Father? Why does every petty little thing kill or crowd out our prayers until we stop praying altogether?

Perhaps this is because we have allowed the things of this life—worries about money, concern about getting ahead in our job, anxiety about our health—to push God out of our center. Perhaps we have become so at home in this world that the world of prayer has become a strange and alien place.

If so, now is the time to rethink our priorities and ask God to become central in our lives once again.

Monday • "When you pray" sounds like clear direction. Christ doesn't say to the disciples, "When you're in the mood" or "When you have time" or "When you need something." He clearly says, "When you pray." Christ explains an important part of our relationship with him.

Think for a moment how it feels to be in the company of a new friend. We like that person and want to spend more time with him or her. We phone and text them frequently. We share our interests and our dreams with that new person in our lives.

To have a closer relationship with Christ, we do the same thing. We talk with him more frequently. We share our interests, our dreams, and our needs. We pray.

Do you think of God in Christ as a friend who treasures you, who wants to be part of your life?

Tuesday • In Matthew 6:5, the Gospel tells us that "The Father knows what you need before you ask." If God already knows, why bother to ask? An earthly father knows what his children need before they ask. But when children are able to be clear about what they need, they and their father have an opportunity to have a relationship. Say a twelve-year-old child wants a new bike. "Dad, can you give me the money for a new bike?" The father knows his son has outgrown his old bike. "I need it for my paper route, Dad!" The dad knows about the new paper route, but when he and the son talk about it, they now work together toward a common goal.

Our heavenly Father also wants to hear about our goals in life. We can share our rationale with him. He wants to be with us as we go forward. When we pray, we become more clear about what we truly need and how our heavenly Father can be with us.

Is there a goal, an anxiety, that you wish to talk about with God? You don't need to wait for the perfect words. Remember, God wants this relationship with you.

Wednesday • Why does prayer sometimes seem like "work"? Why isn't prayer the basis of our joy? Is it because prayer has become an "extra add-on" rather than forming the real substance of our existence?

When we are away from loved ones, we can't wait to talk with them. As soon as parents hug their college-bound children goodbye on that new campus, they anxiously wait to hear from them. "Who are your new friends? How are your classes?" What joy to know they're OK and happy. When our military spouses and parents are off to war, we can't wait to hook up with Skype to see that they are safe and to talk—about anything at all.

When we pray regularly, that joy in connection with Christ becomes more and more part of our daily lives.

What practice of daily prayer brings you the joy of relationship with Christ? When you find yourself making progress in overcoming an anxiety, an attachment, or an addiction, do you stop and thank Christ for his involvement in your life? Do you find joy in the gift of progress he is giving you?

Thursday • Prayer can seem like a strange and alien place. Sometimes we haven't taken the time to seriously pray since childhood. We don't even know where to begin. Those "formula" prayers we learned as kids seem far away now. But those formula prayers might be a place to begin. I remember restarting a daily prayer life with a morning offertory prayer from childhood. "I offer thee my prayers, work, joys, and sufferings of this day." It seemed oddly comforting, and I was able to put in some particular requests at the close of it. I began saying it as I drove to work, and though that later seemed to be just fitting God into my spare time, it did get me thinking about prayer.

How might you be more intentional about prayer?

Friday • Remember the parable of the king who prepared a feast and sent his servants to gather the invited guests? The people on the guest list gave all kinds of excuses for not being able to attend. "I'm too busy," "I just got married," "I just bought a new field and I've got work to do," so they missed the banquet! We are those guests. We are too busy with work, with soccer practice, with laundry, and we miss the feast. We miss prayer. We miss teaching our children about prayer. We miss the connection. And we miss Eucharist—the ultimate feast!

What are you missing out on? Do you feel you'd like to be invited to a feast?

Saturday • When the disciples asked Christ how to pray, he gave them a perfect prayer—a prayer that honors who God is and allows us to ask God for the things we need. He's ready to provide the things we need to be in relationship with him. In the next week we will explore that prayer. We will think about honoring God and the petitions outlined for us to be in that relationship.

The prayer is the Our Father, or the Lord's Prayer, and it starts, "Our Father, who art in heaven, hallowed be thy name." Start thinking about what that means for you. How is God your parent? Do you think of God as loving and caring or stern and demanding? Might God be a divine Being who is ready to give even more than you are ready to ask? "Who art in heaven"—does that put God somewhere up in the sky, or is God here, next to you, listening to your every word every minute, day and night? "Hallowed be thy name"—holy is your name!

How do I pray this prayer? Do I think of God as my loving parent? Am I really God's child?

Week 40: Honoring God's Name

Hallowed be thy name.–MATTHEW 6:9

Sunday • The Lord's Prayer is so familiar that we sometimes race through it without thinking about what we are saying. It would be helpful to slow down and think about the petitions.

The first petition is "hallowed be thy name." What are we asking for here? On the surface we are asking, "Let your name be made holy." But what does that mean? God's name is already holy. So does this make any sense?

Actually it turns out that we are the answer to that question. As people who, in Christ, belong to God, we bear his name. We received his name in baptism...Christians. That makes us Christ's representatives on earth. Whatever we do in our daily lives reflects on God's name.

When we are loving toward others, when we work to heal the brokenness of others, when we are gentle with our spouse and patient with our children, like a mirror, we reflect God. Every day we have wonderful opportunities to "be" his image, to carry his name. That's how we help to "hallow" or "make holy" God's name.

Monday • Many of us learned the words of the Our Father as children. We don't usually give it much thought, but the entire prayer reflects our relationship with God and it starts out with his name—God in Christ. That's the community to which we belong.

How can we be sure about that? Because in this prayer, this "family prayer," we are honored to have been baptized into it, whether as a child or an adult. We are claimed. God knows our name. When we hear the baptismal words naming another person as a Christian, they are welcomed with the sign of the cross. The priest turns to the congregation and says something like, "Please say hello to the newest Christian." It's a way of remembering that God says "hello" to each of us every day.

Do you remember your baptism? Did your parents tell you stories about it? Do you renew your baptismal vows? Do you experience your name of Christian as naming your relationship with God in Christ?

Tuesday • When we identify God's name as holy, or hallowed, we have a responsibility to honor it. We have a responsibility to not disgrace it by using it casually or as an expletive. In the grocery store I saw a child attempting to get gum from a vending machine. The gum wouldn't come out, and the mother was becoming more and more agitated. The child was OK, but the mother was acting out! After a moment she exclaimed, "Good God, I really don't care about your gum!" She said this without thought. "Good God!" Of course God is good. But in this case not only was she disgracing God's name by not realizing what she was saying, but she was teaching her child to do the same. We get enmeshed in bad habits without any real intention to dishonor God. We just forget "hallowed be thy name."

Listen to yourself and those around you. How is God's name used?

Wednesday • We have a responsibility to honor God's name. How are we to do that? We honor it by living lives of discipleship. *Discipleship* can be a pretty intimidating word. I rarely feel like a disciple. I know I fall short. I get absorbed in my own little desires and priorities.

But discipleship really isn't that complicated. It means paying attention to the needs of others. It means having eyes that see the needs of others. It means having ears that hear the needs of others. It means having feet that respond to the needs of others. A friend of mine is undergoing her fifth round of chemo for ovarian cancer. I mentioned her before. When our area was hit by terrible flooding, with roads ruined and homes washed away, Karen was in full operational mode. She organized her local church and worked within her diocese to respond to the immediate and long-term needs she saw around her. When asked why she was so involved, her response was, "Because of Christ."

"Hallowed be thy name."

Look around you today. Who in your family needs an encouraging word? Is there someone in recovery you haven't seen for a while? Reach out. Be a disciple.

Thursday • When we admire or respect a person, when we think of someone as a good person, we expect certain behavior. If we then hear that this person has engaged in behavior that is immoral or illegal or even just rude, we begin to question who that person really is at his or her core. We wonder where the behavior came from. We wonder if we even know the person.

Do we know who we are as Christians? As Christians, we are told that we are made in the image of God. We are told that at our core God in Christ is with us. Have you ever really thought about what that might look like? Again that comes with an amazing responsibility. We are to honor that image.

Do people see a reflection of Christ when they look at you, when they watch your behavior?

Friday • To honor God's name in Christ, to live as disciples, to reflect God's image in our lives, we must pay close attention to the name of God. We can't pray "hallowed be thy name" without taking action. It is not just some passive greeting. It invites an awareness of the things we say, the things we do, and the decisions we make. It demands a focus in our lives to think things through with the ever-present question, "Is this the most loving thing I can do?" That is what Christ asks of us—that is what reflects his image—to love one another.

Is there an opportunity to honor God's name today? At the close of today, take time to consider where you honored God's name. Did it bring you pleasure? Was it a bit more of a reaching out than is usual for you? Do you think the other person noticed? What makes you think that?

Saturday • When we reflect God's image, we take on discipleship. It's a new way of living, a new way of being. Where do we get the call to engage in this new life? Where do we get the power to make the subtle and not-so-subtle adjustments in who we are?

We get it all from God in Christ. We receive it as a gift. We don't make these changes ourselves just because we think they are a good idea. They are a gift from Christ. The power to change comes from Christ. We ask for his power. We ask for the Holy Spirit to be with us on a daily and moment-by-moment basis, to guide us to honor God's name, to reflect that Godlike image, to love one another.

There is nothing the Holy Spirit likes better than to be asked, to be invited into our lives.

Is there a special challenge in your life today that you want to invite the Holy Spirit to help you with? Is there a project at work that is causing you stress and you need help to be considerate of others' stress? Is your child experiencing a problem and you need to take time to show love and support—to honor God's name, to love one another? "Hallowed be thy name."

Week 41: Abundant Life

Thy kingdom come.–MATTHEW 6:10

Sunday • We want Jesus' kingdom to come to us. We want him to rule our hearts and our lives. But do we really? That can be a problem if we've allowed other things to sneak in and take control. After all, we're used to making decisions without asking God's opinion.

Often Christ does not occupy first place in our lives. We make plans, set goals, and establish priorities as though God doesn't exist. Our attachments and our addictions call the shots. They are the tyrants who daily seek to control us.

When we pray "thy kingdom come," we are asking that these tyrants, these false gods, be cast off the thrones they have set up in our hearts and lives and that Jesus Christ take control.

That's a good thing! Jesus Christ is not a tyrant. He is a loving and gracious ruler. He wants to replace our anxiety with his peace, our shame with his forgiveness, our weakness with his strength, our despair with his hope, our loneliness with his presence. When Christ enters our hearts and lives, that's when we experience the abundant life.

Monday • This week we consider what we really mean when we pray, "Thy kingdom come." This part of the Lord's Prayer asks us to move from our consuming focus on our lives to a place where we can consider God's good and gracious rule in our hearts. Normally, we get up in the morning and start full throttle on what we have to do, where we have to go, and with whom. Then we organize our other priorities of exercise, fun, and friends. It's very easy to get overwhelmed by the tyranny of our self-importance, our busyness, our stress, our anxieties, our attachments, and our addictions. We wind up serving them rather than having them serve us. We take little time to consider how all this fits with the kingdom of God.

And then if we are open, this wonderful miracle occurs. We begin to pay attention to another way of being. We begin to be open to Christ in our lives.

Are you aware of a miracle occurring in your life? Do you see a way for the stress, anxieties, attachments, and addictions to take less control in your life?

Tuesday • Though we pray for changes in our lives, for less stress, for a more meaningful relationship with God, we get a bit concerned about what that might mean. All this stress and pressure seem to give some meaning, some importance to our lives. Have you noticed when you ask people how they are, they will usually first say, "Oh, fine." But very quickly you hear all about their stress, all the things they have to do, their lack of time to do it all, and how important they are!

When we begin to pray, really pray, for a new life, for his gracious reign in our lives, we get a little nervous. Is this new life going to be boring? Will we be diminished? Is our life, our self-importance, going to be drastically changed?

Most likely, things will change, but it will be for the better. For those of us with addictions, there is the concern or real fear of who I'm going to be, what I will do for fun if I really move into recovery, into God's kingdom. Those are the same concerns for folks who have attachments to money and career—to anything that identifies who they are. Attachments keep us from God's kingdom.

What are you really praying for when you pray, "Thy kingdom come"? Is there a little hesitation? Do you qualify that petition? Do you wonder what that might mean?

Wednesday • Does your image of who God is make you somewhat hesitant to give him total permission to establish his rule in your life? Are you concerned that God is an angry, controlling tyrant who might take all the fun out of life? Are you concerned that God's kingdom might cause you to feel full of guilt and shame for all your past sins?

In asking God for his kingdom to come into our lives, we are displaying our trust in a Father—the One we have just greeted as holy. We are displaying our trust in God's promises of hope and peace. We are displaying our trust that God will give us his power to be true disciples.

Sometimes the moments of God's kingdom are so subtle. I have a close friend whose 54-year-old husband has been diagnosed with early onset Alzheimer's. It is truly a tragedy for all. I was with them at church a few months after the diagnosis, and after the Sign of Peace, Doug and I continued to hold hands tightly for several minutes. I raised his hands to my lips and kissed them. In that intimate gesture, God's kingdom was present and alive—for both of us.

Is there one thing today that would make you more aware of God's kingdom actually coming into your life? Could it be something in nature? Could it be a step in healing a relationship?

Thursday • When God grants us his kingdom, he promises us a life of abundance. He came to give us life and give us life abundantly. What does living life abundantly mean? Does it mean we'll never feel the grip of scarcity again? Does it mean we'll live with more than we need? That's exactly what God desires for us—a sense that we have more than we need. He's not talking about winning the lottery or having lots of shoes or trucks. God is talking about an awareness of his grace, his love. In his kingdom we have an abundance of his forgiveness, of his gracious love, and of his always being present.

When we live always mindful of how rich we are, we'll experience a life of peace, free from attachments and addictions that rule us. In his kingdom, fear is not the dominant note.

What does living in abundance mean for you? If you could rest in God's kingdom, what fear would you be rid of?

Friday • When we live the abundant life, a life in the kingdom of God, we lack nothing. In fact, we have so much that we can freely give to others. Our hearts are so filled with the spirit of Christ that there is simply no other way to live. We are free to put our past behind us. We can trust the promise that says, "He knows your sins no more." When we live from this "kingdom place," we will notice what needs to be done. We'll make that phone call to a friend in trouble, we'll stop to chat to someone on the street, we'll say the loving word in an argument.

The kingdom of God is a joyful life. It is so overflowing, we are free to share it with others.

How do you share your abundant life? How do others around you know you live in Christ's gracious kingdom?

Saturday • It is through God's power and graciousness that we become aware we are living in God's kingdom. His kingdom has truly come for us. And as with all his gifts, he wants us to participate in the miracle of this gift. He wants us to delight in this kingdom and to share it with others. We are not to hide this gift. Have you ever heard the parable of the "talents"? When they're used and invested, they multiply. One servant buried his, and the returning master was not happy. Resources are to be used, not hoarded. And if our "talent" is the knowledge of God's kingdom, then we simply can't hide that gift.

How do you share the knowledge of this gift of God's gracious presence in your life? Are you willing to share how you pray?

Week 42: A Relationship of Trust

Thy will be done.–MATTHEW 6:10

Sunday • This is not an easy request. We are asking that God's will—not our will—be done in our lives. Who wants to give up their own will? There is a part of all of us that is far too stubborn and rebellious for that. "No one's going to tell me what to do! I'll live my life on my own terms, thank you very much!"

But in this petition we ask that God's will be done—not our own. We ask for God's strength to be able to live life on his terms.

A key issue here is the spirit in which we pray this petition. We can pray it with a spirit of resignation or we can pray it with a sense of duty. And there's a third alternative. We can pray it with a spirit of joy and willingness. Jesus is the one who taught us to pray this petition, and he wants only the very best for us. He wants us to experience a life that is full and rich and abundant.

Monday • Uh oh! I'm not sure I'm ready to pray these words. For many of us who grew up in a chaotic family (and who didn't?), "my will" tends to be the bedrock of who I am. Having control over my life seems essential to my own security. It is who I am. "After all," we might think, "if I can't plan, predict, and control it all myself, what will happen? I may not be safe."

Rather than pray "thy will be done," I'd much rather pray, "As much as I love you, God, I'm just not really certain you are paying attention to what's going on here. So if you don't mind, I feel I have to be very cautious about what might be your will and what is my own best interest."

In our daily lives, God's will might feel like giving up our right to live our life as we see fit. It might feel like giving up our right to be right. In the middle of an argument, in doing my will, I might find myself thinking, *I'm not sure I'm the one who has to apologize here!* Or at another time, *I'm not sure I need to give up all the drugs—maybe just the illegal ones.* When all is said and done, we're just not sure what God's will gets us.

What do you accomplish with your own will? How do you feel about asking that God's will be done instead?

Tuesday • When we think about asking that God's will be done rather than our own, we are asking for God's grace to help us begin the process from "letting go" to "trust." What are we letting go of? We're letting go of our fears and anxieties, our attachments, anything that interferes with our relationship with God. And of course, the biggest one of all: letting go of the need to feel we are in control. After all, in our hearts we know we are not really in control; but we continue to think we have to be.

So we're asking for much more than help to "let go." We're asking to enter into a relationship of trust. In that new relationship, we trust in God's love. We trust that God knows what is best for us and that it will bring us peace.

Sometimes it is very difficult to see God's will in our lives. When we experience illness and sadness for ourselves or those we love, it is so difficult to say, "Thy will be done."

Do you struggle with praying this petition? When? How do you talk with God at those times?

Wednesday • When we struggle with this petition, it might be for any number of reasons. We might say to God, "Why bother to pray this? You are the one with all the power here. You'll do what you want anyway." So we pray with a sense of resignation. Or we might pray it grudgingly. We are like teenagers whose parent still has most of the control and the teenager resents everything the parent says or does because of that.

Or maybe we pray this out of a sense of duty. If we fail to see that God only wants the best for us, we know we should pray this, but it doesn't feel sincere. If we don't sense a loving relationship with God, we pray "thy will be done" with an attitude. It's like showing up for Thanksgiving or Christmas dinner as a duty, but you can't wait to get out of there. You have no real interest in connecting with your family.

Is this petition uttered out of a sense of resignation or duty? What do you resent? It's OK to name it. God wants to talk with you about it.

Thursday • If we pray "thy will be done" out of a sense of resignation, duty, or resentment, we say the words in a cheerless, lifeless manner. They come out with a sense of emptiness. If we hold on to our need to be in control, we continue to live, not in his kingdom, but in turmoil. We are living a life without trust.

But what God wants for us is an abundant life. He wants us to live an authentic life. He wants us to know our strengths through his power. He wants us to know how the struggle for control interferes with our ability to enjoy his gracious goodness.

God loves us. He wants to laugh with us about where this need to control gets in the way of our life, and particularly in our life with him. In our daily life, this need to control interferes with all loving relationships. In our relationship with God, it interferes with our trust in his love for us.

How do you feel when others don't trust that you have their best interests at heart? What might happen in your life if you recognized God's will operating fully and lovingly?

Friday • "Thy will be done" brings us comfort even when we're sick or sad. When we are able to pray "thy will be done" with trust, we encounter these challenges with less need to have all the answers. When we begin to "let go," we begin to feel a freedom, a lessening of tension. We begin to say, "I don't have to have all the answers." When we can honestly say, "I can trust in a loving God whose will for me will hold me," we feel a quiet, a cheerfulness, a fullness.

Who in your life would be most pleased to be aware of your movement into prayer of "thy will be done"? Who would see the difference?

Saturday • Ultimately, "thy will be done" brings a sense of peace. Christ said, "My peace I bring to you; my peace I give to you." That is one of God's greatest desires for us—that we live in peace and that we begin to trust the peace "that surpasses all understanding." That, in effect, is the ultimate prayer in the words "thy will be done." Sometimes we don't understand God's will, but when we trust that he is a good and gracious God who treasures us and holds us in his embrace through it all, then we begin to say "thy will be done" with hope.

What would you hope for when God's will is accomplished in your life?

Week 43: Basic Needs

Give us this day our daily bread.–MATTHEW 6:11

Sunday • "I need bread." By admitting this, we're saying we can't get "bread" ourselves. We're dependent on God. That's what makes this petition another tough one to pray. What makes it so difficult is that we like to think of ourselves as self-reliant and self-sufficient. We're independent, and we want to stand on our own feet with little or no help. We find it difficult to admit that we are powerless over our attachments and addictions.

But the truth is, God has given us everything we need to live. And we are to be, as the Apostle Paul says in his Letter to the Philippians, content with that. "I have learned to be content with whatever I have. I know what it is to have little, and I know what it is to have plenty. In any and all circumstances I have learned the secret of being well-fed and of going hungry, of having plenty and of being in need. I can do all things through him who strengthens me" (4:11–13). When we pray, "Give us this day our daily bread," we are saying, "God, you are the one who makes my life rich."

Monday • When I prayed this as a kid, I thought I was asking God to give me toast and peanut butter and jelly sandwiches—food for that day. My family was never without food, so it didn't make sense to me. Then when my dad lost his jobs time after time, I realized the great anxiety in our house about how the bills would get paid, where the food would come from, where we would live next. Those kinds of childhood anxieties never go away. They have colored many decisions in my life—some positive and some negative.

Now when I pray these words and concentrate on the word *give*, I'm thinking about whether I accept God's grace and power in every part of my life. Do I "take in" what God gives me? This petition reminds me daily that God has the ultimate power to give. All I need do is accept all I need. I have all the physical things I need to live. I know this deep down, so those childhood fears and anxieties no longer serve me. I can open my heart now, knowing I'm protected—and loved.

Do I understand "give" as a pleading for God to be involved in my life? Do I open my heart to accept what I ask him to "give"?

Tuesday • In this petition, if we take "this day" in a very literal sense, it means God is telling us to offer our petitions daily. He wants to hear from us every single day. Isn't communicating daily to our loved ones a wonderful part of our intimate, loving relationships? A young friend recently moved away from the city in which her parents live. She said, "My mom misses me so much. We talk every day, but sometimes I'm so busy, it seems like I don't have time to stay in touch that much." Sound familiar? We move away from God, get involved in our own lives, and forget how much God misses us.

"This day" will I remember to offer my petitions, to go to God for help? Will I remember that God longs to hear from me?

Wednesday • When we ask God to "give us this day," the petition could end right there. Just give us this day! None of us has any idea how our day will unfold. Most of our lives unfold slowly with small insights and small decisions over time. But the more we become aware of the choice to ask God daily, to petition God daily to help us be aware of the Holy Spirit in our lives, the more power we have to make loving changes. Each day we get to choose.

Scripture reminds us that the Israelites, en route from Egypt to their Promised Land, received manna from heaven daily when they asked. They were hot, tired, and frustrated. And they received only enough manna for each day. Each day they petitioned for more, and every day it appeared. He promises to hear us daily as well.

Will this day be the one in which I make a change in my behavior that leads me closer to discipleship, to making loving choices? Will this be the day?

Thursday • If we were blessed enough to go to a religious elementary school or have parents who prayed with us daily, we remember how safe we felt. We knew where to go for help. But we also knew we couldn't stockpile God's gifts. We knew by our rituals of daily prayer, Eucharist, and community that God in Christ was the great giver of everything we could ever need—day by day by day. That faith became imprinted on our souls.

If we did not have this childhood experience, then we may need to form new habits of daily prayer. It's just a matter of inviting God every day to help us. We may need to explore what we mean when we ask God for our "daily bread."

As mature adults, when we ask for "our daily bread," we ask God for whatever we need in life to be a loving person. Of course, having our basic needs met can be part of that need. But much more than our basic needs is the yearning we have for the power and grace to reach out to others.

What do you need today as your "daily bread"? What do you ask God to give you this day so that you are an image of his love to others?

Friday • When we acknowledge our dependence on God to give us our daily bread, there is a reciprocal responsibility of gratitude. In this act of gratitude, we are telling God we know we are totally dependent on his love, his generosity, and his promise. And we are grateful—not only that he gives us all this but also that we know it is all from him.

When we neglect to thank God for the gifts and the knowledge of our dependence on him, we get caught in a sense that we alone have the power to change our lives—that our lives are totally up to us. When we thank God for "our daily bread," we remember, "We do all things through him."

When do you remember that you accomplish nothing without God's grace and power?

Saturday • When we ask God for things, we may think, "This sounds like the 'I want, I need' voices coming from our own whiney children." But unlike parents of demanding kids, God doesn't get frustrated or irritated. He doesn't hear, "Gimme, gimme." Instead, he knows us inside and out. When we pray, "Give us this day our daily bread," God hears beyond the "I want, I want" that we parents have heard so often. Instead, God hears what underlies our asking. He knows what we believe to be important. God's patience with us is infinite.

Praying may sound like very serious business, but asking for our daily bread is filled with joy. Like happy children playing, we revel in our abundant lives. We eagerly ask for what it takes to be loving spouses, caring coworkers, good neighbors. When we pray, we sense God's presence with us in the fun and creativity we are having. We can ask God for whatever strikes us as wonderful—good weather, a luscious meal, moments of peace. He wants to hear all those petitions, for he knows they are important in our lives.

What is the "bread" you need today? Is it the courage to try something new? Is it the patience to improve a new skill? Is it a sense of humor so that you do not take yourself quite so seriously? Is it the capacity to laugh more?

Week 44: Forgiveness

Forgive us our trespasses, as we forgive those who trespass against us. –MATTHEW 6:12

Sunday • What's the cost of forgiving someone? It cost God the life of his Son, Jesus Christ. Forgiveness isn't cheap. And it isn't easy. We might have to give up some of our pride. We may have to really think about what's truly important. We might even have to give up our resentments, grudges, and our unholy desire to get even.

But if we're clear that we want to be a disciple of the risen Christ, then it's absolutely essential to forgive those who have wronged us. We all have been hurt at some time or another. Now what do we do about it? Will we hold on to that wound or will we choose a new relationship?

When we pray, "Forgive us our trespasses as we forgive those who trespass against us," we're asking for a new way of living—a new relationship with those who have hurt us and a new relationship with God. So, what are we really asking for? We're asking God to help us forgive others so we can reflect the risen Christ, who daily and richly forgives us.

Monday • When we ask God to forgive us, we name how we've hurt others. When we put a name to something, it makes it real. Then we spend time thinking about our unloving actions or our harsh words. In our liturgies, we use the words, "I confess to almighty God and to you, my brothers and sisters, that I have greatly sinned." We name our sins and we spend time thinking about whom we've hurt because of them. We are expected to come to the Eucharist having confessed those sins with humility and a profound intention of not committing them again.

The relief of confessing those sins, asking for and receiving forgiveness for them brings a flood of joy. A confession within a discussion of one's life and one's struggles gives one a sense of being touched by the Father. It gives a sense of being held and being heard.

Do you experience the relief and joy of confession? Do you believe you are deeply loved and deeply forgiven?

Tuesday • Our anger and resentment make the second part of this petition—"as we forgive those who trespass against us"—more difficult. Long-standing pain can keep us from praying this petition with sincerity. The anger can be toward ourselves for our behavior or toward someone who offended us. When we feel guilt and shame for our own behavior, or if we've been betrayed and abused by someone else, it's difficult to move to a place of forgiveness. But for us to pray "forgive us as we forgive others," we must come to accept that we cannot go back. We can only go forward. This is now our "new normal." And this new way of living is not completed in a single act. Forgiveness is a process. When we name the pain of the past, we are able to say, "Yes, that was part of my past. Whatever the consequences of that event were, and maybe still are, this is my life now."

In the following days of this week we will focus on the model of forgiveness outlined by Desmond Tutu. Rev. Tutu, a black man, was imprisoned, beaten, and abused for years by the white government of South Africa. His model of reconciliation and forgiveness can be used as a guide as we consider God's forgiveness of us and his expectation that we forgive others.

Do you have anger or resentment that you are having difficulty moving past? Can you name the pain?

Wednesday • If we say to a well-meaning friend, "I'm really angry about this!" that friend might say, "Well, you need to forgive and forget." How do we forget? It's not possible. Desmond Tutu says we need to remember. If we try to forget, we run the risk of repeating the behavior. We stuff it so deeply that we may not recognize the impact it has on who we are and how we behave. That is especially true if the anger and hurt come from an incident or pattern of abuse. If we "forget," we run the risk of abusing someone we love—maybe not in the exact way we were abused but in something equally destructive.

It's healthy to remember the anger and the pain—especially if we've aimed it at ourselves. We need to remember our addictions if they have offended God or our families and friends. We need to remember and not excuse it. We need to acknowledge how we've distanced ourselves from God and those close to us and bring it all into our "new normal."

What would your "new normal" look like if you could begin to hold God's forgiveness in a new way? Would that make a difference in how you might begin to forgive others?

Thursday • Another part of the process of resolving anger and moving to forgiveness is to hold those who have "trespassed against us" accountable for their behavior. That means to forgive, we do not have to say, "Oh, that's all right." Instead, we can learn to say, "That behavior caused me a lot of pain. I am incredibly angry and hurt by what you have done." Part of healing from the anger is to be able to acknowledge that a person has acted immorally, illegally, or unethically. Whether the offense is reportable to authorities is something that must be evaluated. Whether you confront the other person is also a decision you must consider and decide how you might do it in a loving way. When we move through anger toward forgiveness, we discover we are not powerless. We have God's grace and power with us.

But we also need to remember that God holds us accountable for our sins. Though his love is unconditional and his forgiveness is his promise of redemption, we are held accountable for our behavior. We are accountable and responsible to acknowledge our sins, to ask God's forgiveness, and to reconcile with those we have offended.

Is there someone you have hurt or angered? To whom do you need to say, "I am so sorry; is there a way we can work through this?" That can be very difficult to do, but you will feel ever so joyful when you have done it.

Friday • When we have offended or hurt someone, we usually have a boatload of excuses. "Well, she did this or that to me," or "He's been acting like a jerk for a long time. I'd just had it."

And when someone has made us angry, there's a good chance there is another side to the story. The other sees the situation from his or her own perspective with his or her own ideas of who was right and who was wrong. Rev. Tutu encourages us in the process of forgiveness to have empathy for the other person's behavior. We are to try to "walk in their shoes," see the bigger picture, imagine what they are going through. We each hold a unique perspective. In realizing this, we can hold them accountable and *still* understand they have a different way of seeing things. It's likely they have different values, different beliefs.

When we offend God and ask for forgiveness, we can be sure God understands what happened to us. God knows our weaknesses, our humanness. He understands what prevented us from doing the loving things. God knows what got in the way of our acting like a disciple. And God forgives us for all of that.

As you work toward the forgiveness of others, are you able to step back and consider what might be going on in their lives? Where might they have learned the behavior that hurt you?

Saturday • One of the most wonderful parts of forgiving others is that when we are able to forgive, we are no longer a victim. When we are able to forgive, the person who caused us anger or pain no longer has control or power over our lives. We are able to give up the need for revenge. We are not consumed with ideas of "getting back." We have a new sense of freedom. We get to write the end of that story.

God promises that he does not remember our sins. While it is not humanly possible to forget our anger, pain, and hurt, God allows us to move through the process of forgiving others. It helps fill the God-shaped void. It is there that we know we are forgiven.

When have you forgiven someone who has "trespassed against" you? Was it hard? What did you learn by doing this? When have you asked for and received God's forgiveness?

Week 45: Personal Demons

Lead us not into temptation, but deliver us from evil.

—MATTHEW 6:13

Sunday • What do you suppose is the greatest evil that could happen to a person: the loss of a child? the diagnosis of a terminal illness? financial ruin? As terrible as these may be, it's none of those things. The greatest evil is to be separated from God. It is to lose contact with our heavenly Parent.

Losing that contact makes all of life very dangerous. The meaning of temptation is to be constantly confronted with the danger of being torn away from God. If we think of temptation in terms of slight offenses and minor lapses and human mistakes and poor judgments, then we have a misunderstanding as to how subtle and insidious evil is. Any time or place the risen Christ is pushed out of the center of our lives, there is a space of evil. That is the God-shaped void.

That is what is so important about this petition. In it we are pleading with God to help us keep him at the very center of our hearts and lives. This is a petition God is delighted to answer. He wants nothing more than to live at our core!

Monday • We see evil in the world every day: war, abuse, murder. We pray for God to deliver us and those we love from these outer evils.

But evil can also sneak inside. The Ten Commandments warn of those daily evils and temptations: lying, stealing, wanting what is not ours, adultery, not keeping holy the Sabbath day, dishonoring our parents, having strange gods. These commandments get translated into our current culture and language in very recognizable ways. Words such as consumerism, selfishness, gossip, and addiction name those evils in today's society.

When we are tempted by these inner daily evils and succumb to them, we create layers of anxiety within our souls. We are tense. We feel like we are in a constant struggle. We realize that we are in a struggle with demons as ferocious as tigers, lurking, waiting.

What do you think of when you first think of temptation and evil? Is it something in the world or a struggle within yourself?

Tuesday • In considering our temptations and struggles with our personal demons, we pray, "Lead us not into temptation." We petition God to remove us from the possibility of committing an offense that causes us to be distant from him. And since God expects us to be involved and take responsibility for our lives, it is vital that we name the demons that confront us. These demons are our enemies, and it is essential to know our enemies.

The demons can be such things as to focus on a career that places advancement above God and family—missing family meals, missing Mass, too tired to pray or be with family—or attachment to things such as clothes, televisions, cars, and trucks. Or demons can be addictions: food, drugs, sex. Some of these demons are obvious, some much more subtle.

As a person with a strong family history of alcoholism and my own struggles with that demon, I must be constantly alert for the signs and symptoms that accompany that disease. If I create stress and tension in my life, that demon tempts me. If I want to celebrate, that demon tempts me. If I become angry, that demon tempts me. The alcohol is not the demon: it is the fact that if the disease takes over, I distance myself from God. I do that by becoming irritable and angry at those closest to me—even God.

What are your personal demons? What are the subtle things in your life that become a priority, that you use as an excuse to push God aside?

Wednesday • These demons, these things in our lives that distance us from God, can also masquerade as virtues to us and to others. It is important, really very essential, to name those "virtues" that cause our struggles.

I consider myself a very patient person, a virtue, but when I become irritable or even seethe at someone else's irresponsibility, I create a demon. If I must have an immaculately clean house but create stress and unhappiness with my family to maintain that, I create a demon. If I give generously to charities but in my head resent the donation and what it costs me, I create a demon. If I must have perfect children but badger and criticize them to attain that, I create a demon.

All of these inner demons tempt us, create our own anxieties, and distance us from a peaceful relationship with God.

Are there "virtues" that you are proud of, things you secretly congratulate yourself for? Would others call them virtues?

Thursday • When we are able to name these demons, we begin to heal. When we begin to acknowledge that parts of us are broken, then they can be mended.

The demons that create evil in our lives come from somewhere. We didn't create them out of nothing just to make our lives full of tension and struggle. As we name our demons, it is worthwhile to consider their origin. Often these tendencies to have priorities other than God come from messages from our past or from our current culture. We hear messages or voices in our head that tell us who or what we should be or should do. These demons tell us something is more important, more urgent than our relationship with God.

When you name a demon, can you think through where that message comes from? Who or what tells you in your head that you "should" do a certain thing or be a certain way? What other message would bring you peace rather than temptation?

Friday • When we are struggling with these demons, we pray to God to "lead us not into temptation." Sometimes it feels as if we're in the middle of a war. Demons like battles. When we're busy fighting something, we don't have the energy or will to be in a peaceful relationship with God.

How do we get off the battlefield? What keeps the demon in our lives? The demon wants to be taken very seriously. He is very proud of the control he has gained in our lives and the fear he creates. When we distance ourselves from God, we relinquish the power to overcome these struggles. But when we recognize that God is there on the battlefield with us, we can begin to smile at the problems we have created for ourselves. Our struggles with career advancement, our perfectionism, and our selfish natures no longer have a hold on us. "Deliver us from evil."

Do you recognize the power you have given to a demon?

Are you open to guidance from the Holy Spirit that leads you away from temptation?

Saturday • God loves laughter. "Relax! I am with you!" When we are able to name our demons and laugh at ourselves, the Holy Spirit leads us off the battlefield. God walks right by our side. Smiles destroy the demons. We can be assured that much of our lives, our struggles, our temptations, and the evil in and around us are a mystery, but a mystery in which God promises to be with us.

Laugh much and laugh often. It scares away the demons and reaffirms to yourself and others that Christ is with you and in you.

Advent/Christmas: Season of Hope

The next seven weeks are a discussion of Christmas. This starts before Advent and moves to year's end—a time when Christmas is all around us.

Week 46: Invitation to Christmas

All went to their own towns to be registered. Joseph also went from the town of Nazareth in Galilee to Judea, to the city of David called Bethlehem, because he was descended from the house and family of David. He went to be registered with Mary, to whom he was engaged and who was expecting a child.

–LUKE 2:3–5

Sunday • As Christmas approaches, it is the time of year invitations pile up. There are invitations to the office party, invitations to parents' homes for a Christmas celebration, invitations to friends' homes. We can easily receive a dozen invitations.

The danger in all this is that in responding to all these invitations that come our way, and in which we delight, we can become so busy that we fail to take note of the most important of all invitations—the one that God extends to us. Do you know what is in this Christmas invitation? It's just two words: "Come home."

Are you going to respond to this invitation? Are you coming home for Christmas? Perhaps it depends on how homesick you are. The prodigal son in Jesus' parable in Luke 15 finally got sick of the life in the far-off country and decided to return home. Are you sick of life in the far-off country where life is measured by how much you can accomplish; the far-off country where you struggle with constant failure and defeat; the far-off country where you are required to prove yourself daily; the far-off country where there are constant struggles with your spouse and difficulties with your family?

"Come home" from all of that, Christ says. "Come to me, all you that are weary and are carrying heavy burdens, and I will give you rest" (Matthew 11:28).

Are you going home for Christmas? The invitation is before your heart. The Father's door is wide open. He and his Son are ready to embrace you and welcome you to the greatest Christmas party ever. Go on home! Every day go on home to him who has been born, died, and risen for you.

Monday • What are all those holiday invitations saying to us? They are saying that family and friends want to see us. They want to be with us. They want to spend time with us. They want to connect with us. They want to have a relationship with us.

Unfortunately, there are so many guests at most holiday parties that we really don't get to have a meaningful connection with anyone there. We do the cocktail-party small talk, have a few hors d'oeuvres. We notice the Christmas tree and its decorations, the preparations the host and hostess have made, chat a little longer with the people we know, and then we leave.

Even when we leave those parties with a nice feeling, glad to have been included, we have little sense of having connected with anyone; it's just been a time to say "hello." Maybe that is why Christmas preparations—decorating, baking, and gift-giving—often leave us feeling empty and wondering what all the fuss is about. It's a nice way to say hello, but spending time considering what this glorious, joyful day is really about is not part of the schedule.

What if we mentioned to our friends that the mystery of the

birth of Christ has us in a very meditative, reflective mood? What if we questioned what all this holiday fuss is about?

What makes a festive celebration? What are we really celebrating?

Tuesday • If we truly listen, the music may tell us what this celebration is about. In the coming Advent season, the religious hymn prays, "O Come, O Come, Emmanuel." We pray for Christ to come into our world. We pray for him to be in relationship with us. Without him, we feel empty. That yearning comes through in many popular songs we are already beginning to hear: "I'll Be Home for Christmas," "It's the Most Wonderful Time of the Year," and "White Christmas." Popular holiday songs yearn for the older, quieter times we spent connected with loved ones—in relationship. We know we are in a far-off country, and we pray and sing for connection, for relationship. The songs echo Christ's yearning to be invited back to us.

Have we forgotten he is our most important guest?

Wednesday • Too often we wake up in a "far-off country." We've wandered too far from home. When we grow up and move away from home, the reality is we lose connections with many people we love. As we start our families and careers, we even grow apart from our parents. We're so busy, we miss calling them on a regular basis. A quick e-mail is easier than a letter. Maybe if we get instant messaging, it will feel like we had a visit. Let's hope they check our page so we can rationalize that they keep up with us that way. We talk about getting together for a visit but have to fit it into our work and the children's school schedules. We lose touch. Their voices are tinged by sadness when we do take time to call.

Has that happened to your relationship with God? Have you moved to a far-off country and lost touch?

Thursday • And then your parents' Christmas card arrives. It is an invitation to come home for a visit. It even has round-trip tickets for you and your family. In the invitation they say how much they love you and miss you. They know how busy you have been. They know how demanding your job has been. They know you've spent too much money this year. They know you've been struggling with that family addiction—sometimes successfully, sometimes not. They know all this and more than anything, they want time with you.

If you can't see your way clear to come home, can they come visit you? "We need to have some time together. When you are so far away, we're afraid we will lose you."

Christ sends us a ticket home by his Incarnation.

Friday • The home Christ invites us to is like no other. If we have come from a home where there was constant criticism, abuse, or violence, then an invitation to come home may not be very attractive. But that is not the home Christ invites us to. What is your ideal picture of home? The popular song asks for snow, mistletoe, and presents under the tree. It is a romantic picture of being home for Christmas. And it also paints some beautiful images of the home Christ invites us to—a blanket of white snow that covers our sins; mistletoe where we are held in Christ's loving embrace; and the gift of God's Son, born for us this day.

As Christmas approaches, listen for Christ's invitation to come home...home where you are loved and cherished.

Saturday • Remember the excitement of the first trip home for Christmas after you had moved away, maybe to college, maybe to the city for your first job? You had been so homesick. You packed up presents for everyone and couldn't wait to see your house and have Mom and Dad hold you. Of course television advertisements love to make us think that is how returning home will always be. Unfortunately, that is not always the case. Many things get in the way of the "perfect" homecoming.

Nothing but us gets in the way of our coming home to Christ. We are the only thing that interrupts that trip. The truth is, the far-off country is never too far. The weather is never too severe. Money is never an object. (We go first class!) It is always perfect.

Can you just accept the invitation?

Week 47: Rejoice Always

Rejoice always, pray without ceasing, give thanks in all circumstances; for this is the will of God in Christ Jesus for you. Do not quench the Spirit. –1 THESSALONIANS 5:16–19

Sunday • Advent is a wonderful time of the year. It is the time the Church sets aside to prepare for the celebration of Christmas and to reflect on the great miracle of God's becoming Man so that we might become the children of God! It is a time of quiet and patient waiting for Christ to accomplish his purpose in our lives.

But what are we to do while we wait? In his First Letter to the Thessalonians, the Apostle Paul spells out how we are to spend our time during Advent. The first thing he says is "Rejoice." Saint Augustine said that a Christian "should be an alleluia from head to foot." Is joy a characteristic of our lives? Many Christians seem to live their lives as though they were going to a funeral. How is that possible? Here we are, God's beloved people, upon whom he has poured out his love, upon whom he has lavished his mercy, upon whom he has showered his forgiveness and grace. How can we be anything but joyful?

Monday • The word *advent* comes from the Latin "to come." During Advent we spend time considering who and what is to come. Perhaps we mark this special time by opening one door on an Advent calendar or by lighting one candle each week on an Advent wreath to mark the progression, the "coming" toward Christ's birth. In our Northern Hemisphere, winter days are short and dark—a perfect time for quietly preparing for the coming of Baby Jesus.

This is also the time we prepare gifts to exchange, decorate trees, and find special recipes. These are all signs of anticipation and celebration. Unfortunately in all that preparation of the day to come, Christmas, the "coming" of Christ, we often miss the quiet and the listening. If you have ever been to New York City to see the tree at Rockefeller Center or the window displays at Macy's or Saks, you can be overwhelmed by the crush of the crowds and noise. And yet, even in that noise and crush, there is anticipation. Children's eyes are bright. Parents want their children to see it all and delight...and anticipate.

At this beginning time of Advent, how do you want to spend the time "anticipating"? Can it be a mix of quiet and listening and bright excitement about Christ's coming? How? *Rejoice always.*

Tuesday • What is the reason for all this preparation? We know it is all in anticipation of the celebration of Christ's birth, but what does that birth have to do with our daily life on December 26 and all the days after? That certainly is a question worth considering in our Advent days of quiet listening.

When we are anticipating the arrival of a new baby in our family, there is much joy, excitement, and planning. We dare to dream about the relationship we will have with this child. Christ's birth dares us to dream about our relationship with him and the meaning of that relationship.

There is meaning in all human relationships. Maybe we haven't thought of our relationships that way, but if we consider our close and even our casual relationships, there is meaning. The relationships may have a meaning to do with our jobs. The relationships may have a meaning with raising a family. The relationships may mean to have fun and relax.

What is the meaning of Christ's birth in your life? In this Advent season, can you anticipate a new relationship with him? What would that look like? *Rejoice always.*

Wednesday • Parents anticipating a new baby are joyful. Cribs and blankets and precious clothes are purchased. Parties and showers are given in anticipation of this gift. A mother's eyes are often bright, and she appears as beautiful as she has ever been. Mom and Dad are joyful.

We should be joyful as we wait for Christ's birth. If we are—as Saint Augustine says we as Christians should be—an alleluia from head to toe, then our whole bodies sing "Alleluia, alleluia." Can you hear the angels' echo? Christmas hymns tell us to be joyful—"Joy to the World," "Joyful, Joyful, We Adore Thee."

When you take time to anticipate the coming of Christ into your life, do you have a sense of joy? *Rejoice always.*

Thursday • We were returning to our home in Vermont from New York City by train at Christmas time. A family with seven children boarded after we did, lugging large suitcases and backpacks. Mom and Dad were giving instructions on where the children should sit, and an Amtrak customer-service employee was attempting to get them settled. My husband and I looked at each other with some concern. As the six-hour trip progressed, the children settled down with a minimum of fussing and noise. The parents rarely had to give direction or intervene. I did hear them say they were traveling to Vermont from Florida with a specific hope for the children to see snow for the first time. Their faces were peering out the window in anticipation as the day turned to night.

As the train traveled further north, one of the younger children squealed with delight, "Snow, I see snow!" The others joined in with great enthusiasm, "Snow, snow!" And then the father with a booming voice said, "That's not snow. That's just ice. You could get that much ice out of the freezer at home." He quashed their joy. That is not how our heavenly Father is. Our heavenly Father sits by the window of our lives with us, relishing everything. God is excited with us and enthusiastically encourages us to have fun and to be filled with joy.

That is the meaning of Christ's birth—to give us joy in the knowledge that his love is with us, that the Father delights in us as his children—unconditionally.

If you really believed God delights in you—that you are loved unconditionally and that Christ's birth, death, and resurrection redeemed you—would you have joy? *Rejoice always.*

Friday • A quote, sometimes attributed to Gandhi, sometimes attributed to others, says, "I might believe in your Redeemer if the redeemed acted a bit more redeemed." What do you think the quote is telling us? Is it calling us to act in more joyful ways? Are we filled with joy and willing to demonstrate that we are forgiven and redeemed? And one more thing: Let us remember that anyone who makes us angry or tries to dampen our enthusiasm, like the father on the train, is also redeemed and forgiven. How will remembering this affect our actions?

What might you act like, look like, if you really believe you are redeemed...and so is everyone else? What difference might it make in your daily life? *Rejoice always.*

Saturday • Here in Vermont during Advent, it is dark by 5:00 PM. A relative, who frequently visits in the summer and loves those long days and evenings, visited in mid December a few years ago. She hated the darkness. She has only returned in August. And though I, too, enjoy the long days of summer, this early darkness is a reminder to be quiet and listen. We light the fire and candles. We listen to carols that tell of silent nights and a babe in a manger. The darkness reminds us that a savior will soon be born...the One who brings light into the world.

Listen and pray that this quiet will speak of a new relationship with God, of a new relationship that opens you to the meaning he has in your life. What might that meaning be? *Rejoice always*.

Week 48: Unending Prayer

Pray without ceasing.–1 THESSALONIANS 5:17

Sunday • The second thing we can do while we are waiting for Christmas to arrive is pray. Pray while we wait. "Pray without ceasing," Saint Paul says. How is it possible to do that? We have jobs to do, families to raise, projects to complete. If we spent all our time praying, we would never get anything done.

What does Paul mean when he counsels us to pray without ceasing? He means we are to live our lives dependent on God. Too often we make decisions without any reference to God. We make our own plans, establish our own goals, and create our own dreams as though God does not exist. We are determined to solve our problems, get through our difficulties without any help from God. Someone once said that prayer is giving God permission to help, but we don't want to do that.

Prayer means letting go of the controls. It means turning our lives over to God who has become one of us in Jesus Christ and wants to walk by our side as our friend and companion. To pray is to allow God to be God to us and for us.

Monday • Yesterday's devotion says that to pray without ceasing means we are to live our lives dependent on God. It does not mean we are to be on our knees every minute of the day. Even the brothers at the Weston Priory where we worship have responsibilities that take them into their fields and into town. God truly knows we have responsibilities to family and community, responsibilities that occupy our time and thought.

To pray unceasingly means to wrap our lives in the soft blanket of God's love. The brothers of the Priory have a song entitled, "All I Ask of You Is to Remember Me as Loving You." That is what it means to pray unceasingly—to remember God's unceasing love. He gave us his Son.

Today ask God to give you moments to sense his love wrapping you in peace.

Tuesday • In the busyness of Christmas preparation, is there a way to pray unceasingly? Yes! We make our many tasks sacred.

When we are attempting to find the special gift for our children or our loved ones, we make that a prayer...that we have a moment of inspiration. We see the gift and smile. We know it's right. We wrap it with love. When I was growing up, our family did not value wrapping the gifts. We used last year's paper and sometimes only a ribbon around the store package. These days I see my daughter-in-law taking time with her wrapping. The gifts are lovely. They sit beautifully under the tree, and the anticipation grows. Her love and delight in everyone else's pleasure magnify the gift. Her beautifully wrapped gifts are prayers without ceasing.

When we bake and the aroma fills the house, it is not done because we have to. We do it with the thought and prayer that as the children and loved ones enter the house, they will smile. We pray without ceasing.

When we buy the tree, put it up, and string the lights, we do it because the lights remind us of the "Light that came into the world." We pray without ceasing.

What task today can be unceasing prayer?

Wednesday • We may hesitate at the suggestion that we live our lives dependent on God. After all, our culture holds independence as one of the highest qualities of the mature adult. Why on earth would we pray to live dependent on God? Because we are dependent! We may not recognize it, we may not acknowledge it, but everything we have in this world, everything we do, even who we are is dependent on God.

That can be very difficult to get our head around, as the saying goes. We work so hard to control so much. Again, if we grew up in a chaotic home, we thought we had to control the big and little things. We thought if we were just quiet enough or good enough or excelled enough, the chaos would quiet and no one would notice how crazy our house seemed.

In this quiet time of Advent, we are to consider that we are dependent on God. He does not cause the shadows and darkness in our lives, but he is there to walk with us. If we pray unceasingly, we are aware of his presence. We are aware that he takes our hand and guides us. We are dependent on his love and guidance. The craziness, the stress, and the anxiety quiet.

When you feel the tension and anxiety rising today as you hurry about your tasks, stop for a moment and take God's hand.

Thursday • Parents teach. They teach very young children. They teach teenagers. They hold on tightly. We treasure the connection. And as the children mature, parents remain—always there to hold, sustain in failure, and delight in success…always there to say, "You can do it." If you are a parent, you know. The adult child may not say he or she is dependent on you, but they feel that strong, intimate connection, that relationship. You suffer when they suffer. You have joy when they have joy. You feel such warmth when they say, "I love you." That is a mature relationship. That is adult, human dependence.

Dependence on God does not mean we give up and say, "I can't do it." Dependence on God means a relationship in which we say, "I can't do it my way anymore. I need to listen to your way. I need you to guide me. I need to feel your presence. Teach me. Guide me." To live our lives with the knowledge that we are dependent on God is a good thing. Knowing we are dependent on God places us in relationship with him. Having healthy relationships is another marker of a mature adult.

Where in your life would it be especially helpful to acknowledge that you are dependent on God?

Friday • A vital part of an adult relationship is trust. Trust is dependence. "I am in relationship with you. I trust you. I trust you to be with me in good times and bad. I depend on you to be there." If that is not part of a relationship, there is no relationship. Trust is inherent in a relationship between parent and child, between spouses, and between friends.

Trust in our relationship with God is a way of acknowledging our dependence on him. Trust says, "I depend on you. I know I can trust you to be there." When we become so busy and distracted by tasks, we forget to invite God into our lives. We forget God wants to be included, to be there. God waits outside our door, and we must open it to know his presence. When we pray unceasingly, we become more aware that he is in our life. We open the door.

What Scripture passage reminds you that God is with you at all times?

Saturday • When our state of Vermont was devastated by tropical storm Irene, we learned about dependence. Vermont loves its reputation of independent, self-sufficient people. But once we saw the devastation from the storm, we acknowledged we couldn't fix it by ourselves. On the state level, we sent out a call for help. We depended on neighboring states and the National Guard for help. On the town level, those of us trapped by washed-out roads depended on neighboring towns to clear trails and arrange for food and medication. We couldn't do it by ourselves. We needed resources and people—resources and people who could do things we couldn't do, no matter how independent we thought we were.

We also love to think of ourselves as independent and self-sufficient. But there are things we cannot do alone. We need to send out a call for help. God knows what we need before we ask; all we have to do is open the door. Pray without ceasing.

When does your need for independence interfere with your asking God for help?

Week 49: Thanksgiving

Give thanks in all circumstances. –1 THESSALONIANS 5:18

Sunday • The third recommendation of Saint Paul is to give thanks in all circumstances. A couple of things about this recommendation are worth noting. When we don't feel especially thankful or we feel fresh out of gratitude, our friends often advise us to count our blessings. This suggestion has some validity, but what if we don't feel we have any blessings? What if our health is gone, our retirement funds are depleted, our friends have moved away, or we have problems with our children—then what do we have to be thankful for?

We have Jesus Christ to be thankful for. In him we have

forgiveness and peace and joy and hope. In and through him the control of sin has been broken in our lives. In him we have the strength to give thanks no matter what our circumstances are. We have the assurance of his presence, his promise that no matter how dire our circumstances, he will use them to accomplish his good and gracious purposes in our life. Nothing that happens to us is wasted. In Christ, all things are ours. We have every reason to be thankful, no matter what!

Monday • It is not always easy to "give thanks in all circumstances." This season of Advent is bittersweet for me. My precious, perfect daughter was born on December 22. Twelve years later on June 21, she was killed in a traffic accident. Even many years later, December is filled with memories of the last weeks of pregnancy with her, her birth, and the absolute miracle of bringing her home on Christmas Eve. All of us who have suffered such losses know the incredible grief that overwhelms—even all those years later.

How do we "give thanks in all circumstances"? There certainly are no easy answers to that question. All I really know to do is accept the mystery. Psychologists say the last stage of grief is acceptance. I agree with that in its broadest terms. I have come to accept that there are no real answers to the sadness of missing her. I have faith that God has walked with me in my grief. I have learned God does not cause the pain in my life. In fact, when God saw my grief, he was the first to cry. God holds me now in my sadness. God alone knows that grief.

Would I have searched so longingly for a relationship with God if Merry Pat had not died—or would I have gone along all full of busyness and self-importance?

Do you long for a relationship with God? Do you search for that relationship? How?

Tuesday • In the first years following Merry Pat's death, I could barely listen to Christmas carols. Each visit to the mall or grocery store or even private parties had happy, sometimes inane Christmas music that triggered tears. I counted my blessings that I had two healthy sons, a good job, a marriage that seemed stable, and my health. But counting the blessings didn't fill the void.

As the psychologists also say, "Time heals all wounds." And again I agree with that theory in its broadest terms. Any wound such as a cut or incision or burn does heal in time, but any cut, burn, or incision must also have care and salve and bandaging. All grief needs care and salve and bandaging. Healing takes time, and healing must not be disturbed. Early on, Christmas carols disturbed the healing; now they bring soothing.

What I hear in carols now is hope. I listen to the words and I hear a hopeful, loving message: "A thrill of hope the weary world rejoices, for yonder breaks a new and glorious morn." It is a new and glorious morn—each morn and in my relationship with God. I give thanks in all circumstances.

Is there a grief in your life that still needs healing? Does the grief make it difficult to give thanks? Can there be a "new and glorious morn"? How?

Wednesday • Besides the people in our lives whom we treasure, each one of us values certain possessions. If we lose those possessions, we grieve. One of those possessions we value is our self-image, or self-esteem. If we see ourselves as a good spouse, a good parent, or good at our job, we have an image of ourselves that we value. If that image changes because of some destructive behavior on our part, we lose the image and esteem with which we hold ourselves. Grief is part of that loss.

An acknowledgment of one's addiction or a relapse into any demon can cause that grief. "I am not who I want to be or even who I try to present to the world." In fact, that loss of image is one reason denial of the disease of addiction is such a stumbling block to getting treatment. It is so very difficult to "accept" the reality that I am not who I say I am.

When we can begin to acknowledge that we are losing the value of who we believe we are and who we want to be, we begin to move into acceptance of our new reality. When we can say, "I am addicted to this drug or this behavior, but it does not define who I am," we can begin to heal. We begin to "give thanks in all circumstances." We begin to "fall on our knees! Oh, hear the angel voices."

Can you feel "the thrill of hope"? Can you "fall on your knees" and "give thanks in all circumstances"?

Thursday • It can seem impossible to find meaning in some of the circumstances in the world and in some of the circumstances in our lives. Wars, disease, violence—what meaning can those have? The years wasted because of anxieties and addictions that cause us to limit who we can be—what meaning can those have? And yet in all of those terrible circumstances, stories of goodness and compassion emerge.

The incident of the killing of the Amish girls in Pennsylvania several years ago is one such example. A man entered an Amish schoolhouse, held the girls hostage for several hours, and then killed several of the girls before killing himself. The local, national, and world grief was raw. And yet the Amish community showed the world an example of what faith, compassion, and forgiveness are to be. The first evening following the shooting, a group of Amish men and women visited the wife and family of the killer. We don't know what was said, but their example of gentleness and love stopped us all.

What we do know is that the Amish say the Our Father several times a day. Several times a day they say, "forgive us our trespasses as we forgive those who trespass against us."

Could it be they really believe that? Could it be that at their very core, at the time of a tragic mystery, they are able to put their trust in God?

Could it be they trust God enough to "give thanks in all circumstances"? Do you?

Friday • Another outcome from the incident of the killing of the Amish schoolgirls is the emergence of a new phrase in our vocabulary. The phrase is "new normal." The Amish say they have come to accept the changed circumstances of their lives and their community, the terrible loss of these precious girls, as their "new normal." They don't minimize the tragedy; they accept the tragedy has occurred; they accept their loss and grief and refuse to be defined by it. Their faith has sustained them.

The "new normal" can also be incorporated into the circumstances of our lives—the circumstances for which we are to give thanks—whether we understand them or not. When we acknowledge we have the disease of addiction or that our anxieties keep us from being who we want to be, we have the opportunity to move into a "new normal." We have the opportunity to say to God, "OK, this is a circumstance I do not understand. But I have your promise, your assurance, that you are here with me. I give thanks that I know of your presence in this because you are a faithful God who wants to be with me in this."

Can this belief in God's presence in your life—no matter the circumstance—be your "new normal"? Can you begin to give thanks for that presence?

Saturday • There are moments when I truly want to "fall on my knees": times when I walk into church and see it decorated in splendor to celebrate the birth of Christ; when the soloist begins to sing "Ave Maria"; when the chorus trumpets "Comforter, Redeemer, mighty King!"—can't you hear the "angel voices"?

"The weary world rejoices...the soul feels its worth!" Christmas hymns, in all their splendor, tell us of hope.

What Christmas hymn touches your heart? When you hear it, does your "soul feel its worth"? Do you give thanks?

Week 50: The Spirit's Fire

Do not quench the Spirit. –1 THESSALONIANS 5:19

Sunday • Saint Paul says, "Do not quench the Spirit." Sometimes we feel dead inside. Sometimes we feel empty and bored. At times we feel like we are on a treadmill that is going nowhere. At other times we feel we are in a deep rut that we can't get out of no matter how hard we try. In a word, the fire in our life has gone out. Our friends comment on the lack of life in us—the deadness in our eyes. Where has the fire gone?

The psalmist prays, "Do not take your holy spirit from me" (51:11). Perhaps during this Advent season, instead of complaining that we don't seem to have the Christmas spirit, perhaps we might pray for an outpouring of the Spirit on our lives and in our hearts. The Spirit is the one who enables us to come alive; the Spirit is the one who enables us to pray continuously; the Spirit is the one who empowers us to give thanks in all circumstances; the Spirit is the one who turns on the lights of Christmas and opens our hearts to the wonderful gift of Christ who longs to be born anew in our hearts.

Monday • In these cold, dark days of December here in Vermont, when night comes around 4:30 PM and the temperature falls into the single digits, we build a fire in the late afternoon. To keep that fire going until bedtime takes some tending. At the beginning we use lots of kindling to warm up the chimney and logs. Then we have to keep an eye on it to be certain it doesn't die out. We stir it to give it air and place new logs to rekindle the heat. Our home is an 1850's Vermont cottage and the fireplace is small, built to push the heat back into the room. The living room ceilings are low so the fireplace heat makes the room wonderfully warm and inviting.

It all makes me think of the fire of the Spirit. We must kindle that Spirit. We must stir it in our lives. We must place big logs there to sustain the warmth and heat. Even if you live in Florida or the Southwest, you know the need.

How do you keep the Spirit's fire alive in your heart?

Tuesday • When life feels boring, when Christmas seems to be nothing but work and stress, when we find ourselves complaining about Black Friday and "everyone's" consumerism, it's time to step back. What is going on that we can't think of the joy of the season?

This feeling of boredom and complaining also happens for some people after the initial joy of recovery from addictions and other demons. At the beginning we smile and laugh, so relieved that there is hope—maybe a new way of living and being. Then the reality of life returns. There are still bills to be paid, there is still conflict with our spouse. What is going on that we can't think of the joy of recovery?

Those are the times we need to pay attention to the fire—the fire of the Spirit. We need to pay attention all the time, but especially when our hearts feel cold—when the sun has gone down in our lives, when the temperature of our soul is in the single digits, when all we feel is empty and chilled and all we do is complain about "them." We thank God for his reminder that we need to pay attention to the fire, to tend the flame.

Can you take a few minutes to consider the Spirit's fire in your life today, in this season of Advent? Is it alive? Is it smoldering? Does it need tending?

Wednesday • The signs of Christmas—of the coming of Christ—are all around us. The continuous circle of the wreath reminds us of Christ's never-ending love. The Christmas carols sing of silent nights of reflection, the herald and call of angels, of Mary's Boy Child. Even songs of the more secular variety remind us of love, family, friendship, and magic.

Christmas lights are often the first thing we notice as Christmas approaches. Who has their home decorated first? As we travel at night we see the trees lit in neighborhood living rooms. We don't notice the lights during the day. Why? Of course, because there is daylight, the Christmas lights are muted. But at night they are a sign of Christ's coming. Isn't it interesting that Christ says he is the Light of the world? We see him most clearly when there is darkness—darkness in our lives and in the lives of those we love. But the wonderful news is that his light is there always—day and night.

Don't wait for the darkness to pay attention to the Light.

Thursday • What puts out the fire of the Spirit in our lives? One painful part of our lives that puts out the fire of the Spirit is the difficulty we have with forgiveness. We have talked about this earlier in our meditations, but the themes of anger and forgiveness come up so frequently in our lives that they bear further consideration.

We hang on to old betrayals and resentments as though hanging on to them is going to change something. We hang on to them as though the person we accuse of the betrayal is going to suffer because of our anger. Yet in our hearts we know we are the ones who suffer. We are the ones who lose the Spirit's fire.

One of the ways we move through the anger and toward forgiveness is to pray about it. During Advent we are encouraged to spend more time in prayer—prayer that we come alive again, prayer that our faith in the coming of Christ soothes our angry hearts. This suggestion for prayer is not about some quiet, passive "Woe is me!" but rather, a frontal assault of naming the demon of anger and our lack of forgiveness and crying to God for a change of heart.

Where in your life do you hang on to anger? Today can you honestly ask God for a change of heart?

Friday • This active prayer to let go of our anger rekindles the Spirit's fire in our lives. As we begin to forgive others, we become more aware of God's forgiveness of us. Recognizing God's forgiveness of us leads us into a new life. We feel as though we are coming alive. It is like a match has been set to the kindling and logs in the fireplace.

When we feel that new life, that rekindling of the Spirit, we begin to let go of our shame—the shame that comes from holding on to our anger, the shame that comes from our destructive, hurtful behaviors, the shame that comes from not living up to who God wants us to be. The rekindling of the Spirit in our lives births us anew.

When you have glimpses of letting go of the anger, of moving toward forgiveness, do you have a sense of God working in your life? Are there moments of a new life? Is it Christmas?

Saturday • Inside this sense of being born anew is an empowerment. This empowerment comes from the Holy Spirit and gives us the courage, the strength, and the energy to move into the wonder of this new life. The wonder is about all the ways God shows he is with us—in this beautiful physical world, in the growth and change he helps us make in ourselves, and in our new awareness of our relationship with him.

But just like recognizing him in the wonder of the physical world, we must pay attention to see him in our daily lives. We need to take time in our day to be aware of changes we can make to be more forgiving, to be more understanding of others, to be more accepting of others. The Holy Spirit is what empowers us to make those changes. That is the wonder of being born anew, of Christmas.

Where in your life do you feel empowered to make a change? This might be a very quiet change, but one you know will strengthen your relationship with God.

Week 51: Missing Christmas

And she gave birth to her firstborn son and wrapped him in bands of cloth, and laid him in a manger, because there was no place for them in the inn.–LUKE 2:7–9

Sunday • Did you ever miss an event that was really important because you overslept? Words aren't sufficient to express the disappointment and heartbreak we felt. Few experiences in life are more tragic than missing a terribly important celebration such as a graduation, a wedding, a child's birthday party—especially when there really was no need to miss it.

But that's precisely the danger we face—the danger of missing Christmas. The innkeeper missed it; he missed the birth of the Savior. It was right there, and yet his preoccupation with his business—his fierce and total investment in the life around him—caused him to miss Christmas. If we asked him the reason, he would probably say something like, "Do you know what it's like to run an inn? It's a 24-7 job. There's no end to the work."

How often, like that innkeeper, have we too become burdened by life and all that it involves? We get buried by life, bruised by distress, pinned against the wall by obligation. It would be easy for us to run the risk of missing Christmas.

And that would be tragic. Perhaps we need to follow the example of the Virgin Mary, the Mother of Jesus, who kept all these things and pondered them in her heart. What did she reflect on? She reflected on the gift that God had given to all of us in the birth of Jesus. In him, we receive the gift of hope, of joy, and of forgiveness.

Have a *Mary* Christmas.

Monday • It's Christmas morning, or maybe as you read this it is the week of Christmas. There has been so much going on. We've anticipated it all through Advent, and now it's here. All this preparation is for a celebration, and now the celebration itself is here. We rush around, open presents, prepare and eat breakfast, clean up the wrappings, think about dinner, get our best clothes ready, get to church. It all still seems to require a great deal of effort. Stop. Be still—return to the story behind all the celebrating. We never outgrow it.

What family tradition of yours brings attention to the reason for the celebration? Do you have a manger scene that you spend a few minutes talking about—especially this morning—all week? Do you read the story of the first Christmas, even a few paragraphs, each evening at dinner or as a bedtime story?

Tuesday • When we turn 18 or 21 or 65, we have some pretty significant celebrations! When we have a 25th or 50th wedding anniversary, we have a real party!

Do you remember how the world anticipated the New Year celebration that brought in the year 2000? All over the world as the clocks turned from midnight on December 31, 1999, to 12:01 AM on January 1, 2000, bells chimed, crowds cheered, and much champagne was consumed. There had been dire predictions that computers would fail and we'd be surrounded by chaos. Planes wouldn't be able to fly, traffic lights would stop functioning. Some people, anticipating a world crisis, stocked up on food and water. But none of those dire consequences happened. The world continued in its wonder and its brokenness.

In all of that, how much did you hear about the real significance of the year 2000? How much did you hear that what we were really celebrating was the 2000th birthday of Christ?

Did we miss the party? Do we still miss the party every year? Do we get distracted? Do we sleep through it?

Wednesday • We might miss the party because we miss the opportunities Christ gives us to celebrate and to know the real meaning of Christmas.

Our Christmas celebration often includes a big meal—fancy stuff we don't have most of the year, special dishes friends and family have told us are their favorites. We prepare the quantities and numbers of servings and set the table with a "planned" guest list. Maybe that guest list is just close family, or maybe it extends to out-of-town relatives and friends, to someone alone.

Following the Christmas Eve service this year, I overheard an interaction between a husband and wife that gave me pause. The husband had noticed that an acquaintance of theirs was attending the service alone. After the last hymn he turned to his wife and said, "Maybe we should invite Clare to join us for dinner tomorrow. She might be alone." The wife's immediate response was, "Oh, no. We have way too much to do. We are leaving in two days and have to pack and finalize our list of getting the house ready for the renters. We have to stay on task."

We all try to "stay on task." We get self-absorbed. It becomes all about us. As a result, we miss reaching out to someone else. We miss an opportunity to care about someone else. We miss opening our homes, our arms, and our hearts. We miss sharing the joy and the wonder. We miss Christ.

Is there a way this week, this day, that you can reach out to someone to share the joy of Christ's birth?

Thursday • You know who didn't miss the celebration? The shepherds! Think about it. They knew little of the prediction of the coming of the Messiah. They weren't educated. They didn't socialize with the "townspeople." They were just "poor shepherds who tended their flocks by night." They probably had just finished dinner, settled the sheep down, tended the fire, and pulled up their blankets. Then whoa! They hear angels singing and see stars shining and voices telling them to go to the stable and see the gift that God had sent. They probably wondered what was in the water they had just drunk! But they hurried to town with the angels' words ringing in their heads: "Glory to God in the highest heaven, and on earth peace among those whom he favors!" (Luke 2:14).

They got the message and found the stable and discovered for themselves that all they had been told was true. Then they went back and told everyone this amazing story. "They made known what had been told them...and all who heard it were amazed at what the shepherds told them" (Luke 2:17–18).

Glorify God, live in peace. Is that the message you hear? Do you understand that?

Friday • This message about the shepherds and angels brings big questions to mind. How do we glorify God and live in peace? How do we live the Christmas gift? The gift God gives us at Christmas is the gift of peace: the peace that comes from God's unconditional love, the peace that comes in "understanding," the peace that results from realizing God's forgiveness. We live that wonderful peace daily through the Eucharist, through inviting others to share in our abundance, through repenting of our sins, through forgiving others. We might not "understand" it all, but like the shepherds, we can dare to live it.

This day, this week, can you go to Bethlehem as the shepherds did and "glorify God and live in peace among all people"? How?

Saturday • In Scripture, the Virgin Mother of Christ never says, "Oh, I get it!" She does not say she "understands" the things going on in her life. Remember, she questioned the angel who announced that she was bearing the Child, "How can this be? I'm not married!" And then at the time she and Joseph presented Christ in the Temple, Scripture says, "And the child's father and mother were amazed at what was being said about him" (Luke 2:33). Mary carries within her a sense of wonder—a sense of the wonderful. And like Mary, we continue to ponder these things in our hearts.

Do we take the time to "wonder" and "ponder"? Do we try to figure out more about this incredible gift of God's forgiveness and love? Do we wonder what that would mean in our lives if we really believed, if we really lived it?

Week 52: Unburdened Lives

Joseph also went from the town of Nazareth in Galilee to Judea, to the city of David called Bethlehem, because he was descended from the house and family of David.

And she gave birth to her firstborn son and wrapped him in bands of cloth, and laid him in a manger, because there was no place for them in the inn.

And suddenly there was with the angel a multitude of the heavenly host, praising God and saying, "Glory to God in the highest heaven, and on earth peace..." –LUKE 2:4, 7, 13–14

Sunday • Luke tells us that Jesus was born in Bethlehem. Do you know where Bethlehem is? Geographically, you would say it is about five miles west of Jerusalem. That would be accurate on a map, but spiritually, where is Bethlehem?

Bethlehem is where Jesus Christ is! And where is that? He is where lives are soaked by sin and souls stained by shame and hearts burdened by guilt and twisted by sin.

Bethlehem is where Jesus Christ is! And where is this Jesus Christ? He is where there are folks crushed by difficulties, folks who struggle with frailties and inadequacies and shortcomings—folks who have nothing to show for all their efforts except broken resolutions and unfulfilled promises. He's with people who are tossed about by fears, worried, anxious, and scared, folks who are unable to handle or cope with the stress and change of life. He is where people are at the point of despair and hopelessness and desperation. He is where the dark is the darkest.

That is where Bethlehem is and that is where Jesus Christ is born. What is our response to that? The hymn "O Little Town of Bethlehem" says it best:

"O holy Child of Bethlehem,
Descend to us, we pray
Cast out our sin and enter in
Be born to us today.
We hear the Christmas angels
The great glad tidings tell
O come to us, abide with us
Our Lord Emmanuel."

Where is Bethlehem? It is in your heart when you ask Jesus Christ to enter in and be born again in you today.

Monday • Mary "laid him in a manger, because there was no place for them in the inn."

When there is no room for him in our lives, we are living with shame and burdened hearts. In this week after Christmas and leading to Epiphany and the New Year, it is worth considering this miracle of the birth of Christ, the miracle that allows us to unburden our hearts to sing "Glory to God."

Sunday's devotion says Jesus Christ is where lives are soaked by sin and souls stained by shame and hearts burdened by guilt and twisted by sin. Whoa! We don't often hear words like that applied to our lives. It's hard to hear those words—especially right after Christmas! In this secular, feel-good world, the emphasis is on words that are more psychological than spiritual. To describe the ways we offend one another and God, we use phrases like "poor choices" and "negative behaviors." When we minimize our offenses against God and others by calling them "poor choices" and "negative behaviors," we deny the seriousness of our sins. We deny the pain they cause and we deny our closed hearts—our "no room in the inn" sign to God.

In this week following Christmas day, we are invited to make room for God in our lives, to sing his glory.

Is there an area in your life that is difficult to name as "sin"? Do you minimize the impact sin has on people you love and on your relationship with God?

Tuesday • It takes courage and love to name the sin in our lives. But it takes so much more energy to hold on to that sin, to deny that it is sin, and to deny that the sin has a serious impact on those we love and on our relationship with God. We have to do such mental gymnastics to rationalize the pain and deadness in our souls. We have to tell ourselves such lies to justify the emptiness in our hearts.

When guilt and shame fill the soul, the Spirit's fire is out. But hearing the Christmas story offers us a chance to begin again. Celebrating Christ's birth offers a time to recognize that we don't have to live with guilt and shame. He came to redeem us! There is a new beginning stirring in the world. There is a new beginning for you. There is movement in Scripture. There is movement in the story of Jesus Christ. There is movement in your story.

If you name the sin, if you acknowledge it as sin, can you begin to sense the relief, the peace? Can you begin to hear a new story?

Wednesday • It is difficult to acknowledge what is going on in our lives as sin. We set up blame on the "other." The "other" can be someone else who "did it to us first." The "other" can be those who have more money or possessions and don't share. The "other" can be our child who doesn't call or thank us for the gift. When we focus on the "other," the frustration and irritation we feel interfere with the peace in our soul—the peace that God offered us on Christmas day.

We might not name that lack of peace as a sin, but when we are irritated, worried, anxious, and scared, we are not trusting in the promise of God. We are not trusting that in this miracle of his birth, Christ is fulfilling his promise to be Emmanuel, to be with us. The anxiety, the worry, the fear interfere with the gifts God has given us. In that gift lies the ability to offer the "other" a message of peace. He came for all of us.

Does frustration, irritation, or fear fill your heart? Does that feeling consume you so much that it becomes the focus of your day? Can you begin to name that feeling as sin and ask God to help you let it go?

Thursday • In rural Vermont, winter nights are really dark. There are no streetlights, no light from a nearby town. If I step out of the house into the night, it takes several minutes for my eyes to begin to identify familiar shapes and landmarks.

So it is when we begin to acknowledge that we sin. It takes some time for us to begin to see the shapes and obstacles in our darkness. However once we begin to identify the ways we sin, we can begin to walk forward. The darkness is not as frightening. Even when the darkness is the darkest, Christ leads the way.

Where is your darkness? Can you begin to see shapes and obstacles that keep you from moving into the light...the light of Christ's peace, the light of God's glory?

Friday • If I go outside very early in the morning, often dawn is just breaking. Sometimes the dawn is spectacular with beautiful bands of pink and gold. Then sometimes it is cloudy, and the dawn breaks slowly and gray. Though one is more spectacular than the other, it really doesn't matter which it is. The dawn comes, and the darkness turns to light.

That can be the way it is with our beginning awareness of what Christ's birth truly means in our lives. It can be a glorious awakening to this truth of Christ among us, or it can be a slow "dawning" that the Light does come—day after day after day. Christ's birth promises that he is with us to lead us out of the darkness.

Do you recognize that Christ is born into your life? Can you believe that Bethlehem is in you?

Saturday • In the weeks of Advent, we prayed to follow the Apostle Paul's encouragement and to "rejoice always, pray without ceasing, give thanks in all circumstances, and not quench the Spirit." We prayed to become more aware of this spectacular miracle. As we move into the awareness of God's love for us through the gift of his Son, we are able to move out of the darkness of our sin. We pray that he "descends to us—casts out our sin and enters in—be born in us today."

We sing, we pray, "Oh, come to us, abide with us," and we remember through Scripture that Christ spent time with sinners and people enveloped in darkness. He comes to those in the darkest of dark. He comes to the Bethlehem in us. He comes to unburden our lives.

As we approach Epiphany and the New Year, as you light the candles in your home and see candles everywhere, remember those candles represent the light with which Christ illuminates your darkness. Does that change anything?